Rookwood

A
PRICE GUIDE

EDITED BY
L-W Book Sales

Copyright 1993

L-W Book Sales
Box 69
Gas City, IN 46933

ISBN#: 0-89538-022-6

Table of Contents

Rookwood Pottery
HISTORY

The Rookwood Pottery and the illustrious history that follows it is an inspiration to many. Since the Pottery's inception during the summer of 1880, the influence on contemporary art pottery is obvious. This is clearly understood today, as wares which originated from Rookwood are sought as avidly as artifacts from centuries past. The influence of Rookwood upon the art pottery market during its formative years is clearly shown by the immediate productions released by its competition in the art pottery field. The meticulous care and artistic effort placed into each piece secured an invaluable reputation for the Rookwood Pottery. Fortunately for us, many of these magnificent remnants may still be discovered to this day.

The Rookwood Pottery was founded in the middle of 1880, with the city of Cincinnati as the location. Established by Mrs. Maria Longworth Nichols, its uncertain financial status at its inception was reinforced by the founder's father, Mr. Joseph Longworth. As a patron of the Cincinnati Art Museum Association and the Cincinnati Art Academy, Mr. Longworth made his greatest contribution by ensuring the successful foundation of the Rookwood Pottery. Fueled by Mrs. Nichol's passion for art pottery and design and aided by dependable co-workers, the Rookwood Pottery soon began its steady growth as one of the premiere art potteries of the United States.

Mrs. Nichol's experience with art pottery arose from years of instruction and many hours spent in a studio at the Dallas Pottery, also in Cincinnati. The kilns at the Dallas Pottery, too hot to effectively fire the delicate colors on Mrs. Nichol's painted wares, were later modified to account for the lustrous methods of firing. This was an important task to be done before the origin of the Rookwood Pottery. The Pottery might not have been established if it wasn't for Mrs. Nichol's stubborness in ignoring others in the commercial pottery business that there was not a good enough market for art pottery. This and the threat posed by an early competitor (who attempted to safeguard a patent on the under-glaze process) were bypassed eventually to allow Rookwood to become a spectacular leader in the art pottery market. Thus, on Thanksgiving day in 1880, the first kiln was drawn.

The methods that produced the renowned pottery of Rookwood gained a priceless reputation that carried the company through many ownership and management changes during the next eighty years. Finally, the Rookwood Pottery suspended its operations permanently during the summer of 1967.

Now it's the 1990's and the Rookwood Pottery is still known as the birthplace of many beautiful and unique pieces of clayware. These are the pieces which are still being stalked by many collectors with an eye for the handsome goods which came from Cincinnati's legacy of art pottery.

The Editors wish to thank

Jon Alk
414-435-2211

and

Don Treadway
513-321-6742

for all the
help they gave us
on this book

1

Actual Magazine Ads

All Rookwood Bears This Imprint

ROOKWOOD POTTERY

CINCINNATI

An example of the new glaze produced at Rookwood commemorating its fiftieth anniversary. It is a rich limpid red other than ox blood in character and carries brilliant aventurine crystallization ranging through green, yellow and red gold.

Rookwood may be had through Tiffany and Company, B. Altman and Company and Frederick Loeser and Company, Inc., in the Metropolitan New York area and through an exclusive representative in other cities. We invite your direct inquiry.

August, 1931

All Rookwood Bears This Imprint

ROOKWOOD POTTERY

CINCINNATI

This vase of midnight blue matt, lined with orange, is but one of the innumerable, individual examples coming from the kilns at Rookwood during the past fifty years. Recognized everywhere as supreme Ceramic art, and given the highest international awards, Rookwood possesses the sophisticated charm essential where art meets world-wide requirements in taste.

Rookwood may be had through Tiffany & Co. and The Frederick Loeser Co., in the Metropolitan New York area, and through an exclusive representative in other cities. We invite your direct inquiry.

March, 1930

2

Actual Magazine Ads

ROOKWOOD

For June Weddings

No piece is ever duplicated — every piece is an original painting on pottery, and there is no other like it.

Send for "The Rookwood Book"

which shows many charming designs particularly appropriate for gifts, beautifully illustrated in colors. Its exquisite colorings in soft shades of gray, pink, blue, green and yellow, and its beauty of form, design and glaze have won for Rookwood its worldwide reputation as a work of art.

Grand Prix Paris 1900.
Two Grand Prizes St. Louis 1904

This mark is impressed in every piece *and there is no Rookwood without it.*

Sold by leading dealers.

THE ROOKWOOD POTTERY
1 Rookwood Place   Cincinnati, U. S. A.

June, 1905

ROOKWOOD POTTERY

Supreme technical quality with notable design makes Rookwood distinguished as among the world's greatest ceramics

This artist-signed piece, or one equally choice in color, form and texture will be found at the following exclusive representatives:

Tiffany and Co., Jewelers, New York City; B. Altman and Co., New York City; Frederick Loeser and Co., Inc., Brooklyn; Strawbridge and Clothier, Philadelphia; Marshall Field and Co., Chicago; Schervee Studios, Inc., Boston; L. B. King and Co., Detroit; Brock and Co., Los Angeles; Dulin and Martin, Washington, D. C.; Frederick and Nelson, Seattle. A store of similar quality represents the pottery exclusively in your city. We invite your direct inquiry.

ROOKWOOD POTTERY
CINCINNATI

All Rookwood Bears This Imprint

August, 1931

Actual Magazine Ads

Write for
"The Rookwood Book"

which will take you through the Rookwood Studios, and show you many of the most exquisite designs of the celebrated Rookwood as nearly as possible in their exact colorings.

Rookwood Pottery

received the world's highest honors—**the Grand Prix at Paris, 1900**, over all competitors from Europe, Asia and America.

This mark is impressed in every piece *and there is no Rookwood without it.*

Rookwood is for sale by leading dealers and at the pottery.

Rookwood Pottery, Cincinnati, U. S. A.

November, 1904

All Rookwood Bears This Imprint

ROOKWOOD POTTERY
CINCINNATI

The technical perfection of Rookwood and its artistic quality are acclaimed everywhere, for there are Rookwood pieces suitable to any home or any income.

The horse book ends (illustrated below), in ivory, brown or green Mat Glaze are $10, height 6½ inches. The decorated signed vase is $20.

Rookwood may be had through Tiffany & Co., B. Altman & Co. and The Frederick Loeser Co., in the Metropolitan New York area, and through an exclusive representative in other cities. We invite your direct inquiry.

November, 1930

5

Actual Magazine Ads

Write for
"The Rookwood Book"
which will take you through the Rookwood Studios, and show you many of the most exquisite designs of the celebrated Rookwood as nearly as possible in their exact colorings.

Rookwood Pottery

is the world's most perfect attainment in artistic ceramics, and received **The Grand Prix** at Paris, 1900.

This mark is impressed in every piece **and there is no Rookwood without it.**

Rookwood is for sale by leading dealers and at the pottery.

ROOKWOOD POTTERY, Cincinnati, U. S. A.

October, 1904

All Rookwood Bears This Imprint

ROOKWOOD POTTERY
CINCINNATI

Christmas giving may not be ignored but precious pieces of Rookwood from one dollar and a half up will help solve the problem economically. In the group illustrated below the paper weight in ivory mat, $4\frac{1}{4}$ inches high is $2.50, the modern vase at the back in plain colors is $2.50, with different colored lining $3.00; the candy jar in various colors is $5.00.

Rookwood may be had through Tiffany & Co., B. Altman & Co. and The Frederick Loeser Co., in the Metropolitan New York area, and through an exclusive representative in other cities. We invite your direct inquiry.

December, 1930

Actual Magazine Ad

When You Want
The Wedding Gift

that will give the keenest pleasure and is certain
not to be duplicated, tell us how much you desire
to pay and we will gladly send you by express,
where we have no agent, a selection of pieces direct
from the pottery. You can choose the one you
prefer—remit for it and return the others.

ROOKWOOD
Is The Best Gift

because no two pieces are ever alike—each is an
original painting on pottery—a real work of art
that will always be prized. No illustration can
truly show Rookwood—its beauty of design—decoration, colorings and glaze must be seen to appre-
ciate why it is a work of art.

Grand Prix Paris 1900
Two Grand Prizes St. Louis 1904

The great variety of exquisite new designs ranging in price from **$1.00** to **$500.00** gives an
unusual opportunity for selection.

Send for "The Rookwood Book" which
illustrates in colors many charming designs.

*This mark is
impressed in
every piece* *and there is
no Rookwood
without it.*

The Rookwood Pottery
10 Rookwood Place, Cincinnati, U. S. A.

Rookwood is sold in each city only
by our exclusive Rookwood Agents.

New York	Davis Collamore & Co., Ltd.
Chicago	Marshall Field & Co.
Boston	Bigelow, Kennard & Co.
St. Louis	Mermod & Jaccard Jewelry Co.
	Simmons Hardware Co.
Philadelphia	Wright, Tyndale & Van Roden
Pittsburg	Hardy & Hayes Co.
	Hamilton & Clark Co.
Washington, D. C.	Dulin & Martin Co.
San Francisco	Raphael Weill & Co.
Indianapolis	Chas. Mayer & Co.
Portland, Oregon	A. & C. Feldenheimer
Cleveland	C. A. Selzer
Cincinnati	Loring Andrews & Co.
Toledo	J. J. Freeman & Co.
Atlanta, Ga.	Maier & Berkele.
Denver	Daniels & Fisher Stores Co.
	The Boutwell-Brooks Art Co.
Louisville, Ky.	William Kendrick's Sons
New Orleans, La.	A. B. Griswold & Co.
Columbus, O.	Hasbrook-Bargar Co.
Ithaca, N. Y.	George Rankin & Son
Buffalo	I. R. Brayton
	Walbridge & Co.

1905

7

Actual Magazine Ads

Top ad is from 1904   Bottom ad is from October 1904

9

Rookwood Pottery

has become better known to more people since the book —of which the first cover is here reproduced—telling about Rookwood ware, has been issued. This book explains why Rookwood ware is unique, illustrates many forms and designs of the pottery, and prints the marks by which it can be identified. Copies of the book may be had for the asking from dealers in Rookwood ware, of whom there is one in each of the larger cities, or from

ROOKWOOD POTTERY,
Cincinnati, O

December, 1896

Actual Magazine Ads

Top ad is from June, 1905   Bottom ad is from October, 1905

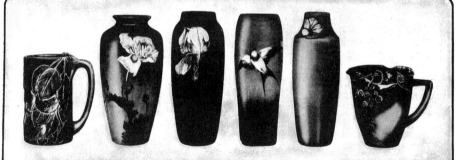

11

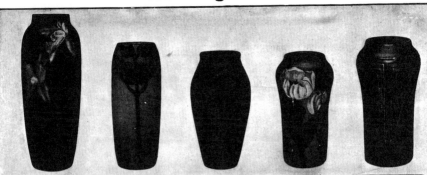

IF YOU WANT A UNIQUE WEDDING GIFT

Of real value as a work of art, something that will always be prized and that cannot be duplicated, send a piece of

Rookwood Pottery

There is nothing more beautiful than genuine Rookwood—its delightful colorings in soft shades of gray, pink, blue, green and yellow—its beauty of form, design and glaze have won its world-wide reputation as a work of art.

Grand Prix, Paris, 1900.
Two Grand Prizes, St. Louis, 1904.

This mark is impressed in every piece **℞** *and there is no Rookwood without it.*

THE ROOKWOOD POTTERY COMPANY, 2 ROOKWOOD PLACE, CINCINNATI, U. S. A.

Top ad is from June, 1906   Bottom ad is from December, 1906

A Christmas Suggestion

YOU give every day in the year when at Christmas you give Rookwood. The charm of artistic beauty is not for one day but for every day, and lasts for all time.

Rookwood is not duplicated

This mark is impressed in every piece **℞** *and there is no Rookwood without it.*

Grand Prize, Paris, 1900
Two Grand Prizes, St. Louis, 1904

Rookwood is sold only by Rookwood agents in each city and at the pottery

The Rookwood Pottery
Cincinnati,   **Ohio, U. S. A.**

Actual Magazine Ad

If You Wish Something Unique

of lasting artistic value, for a gift or for your own home—something that will always be prized—send for a copy of The Rookwood Book, which illustrates by handsome color plates many charming pieces of Rookwood in the different types.

After seeing it you will realize how the incomparable variety of Rookwood adapts it to every environment and makes it the most welcome of gifts.

Potters the World Over

have paid the tribute of imitation to

ROOKWOOD

but its artistic qualities elude them. There is nothing more beautiful in pottery than Rookwood—nothing more worthless than the imitation.

Grand Prize Paris 1900. Two Grand Prizes St. Louis 1904.

This mark is impressed in every piece *and there is no Rookwood without it.*

Rookwood is sold only by Rookwood agents in each city and at the pottery.

The Rookwood Pottery Co.
6 Rookwood Place, Cincinnati, O., U. S. A.

1905

ROOKWOOD

IT is a matter of much thought at Rookwood to produce pottery which has in itself rare elements of beauty and is adaptable to the flowers of all seasons.

Our distributor in your locality may help you in your selection of a piece for the home, or as a gift. We invite direct inquiries.

THE ROOKWOOD POTTERY CO.
Eden Place   Cincinnati, Ohio

October, 1926

14

Actual Magazine Ad

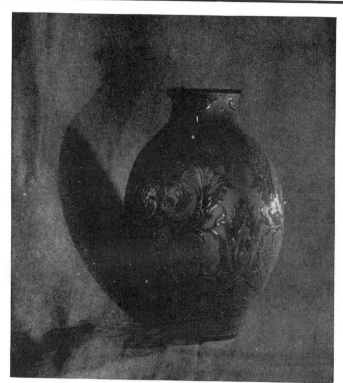

R O O K W O O D

aims at a constant freshness while maintaining the high traditions of an art as old as time. Examine our products which are carried by an exclusive representative in your locality or write direct to us.

THE ROOKWOOD POTTERY COMPANY
Celestial Street, Cincinnati, Ohio

August, 1924

Actual Magazine Ad

ROOKWOOD

There is no gift more appropriate or acceptable than a piece of Rookwood Pottery — few products that make so fine an impression of value for small expenditure.

These pieces are exceptionally lovely in ivory, lined sky blue and soft burnt orange with turquoise; but many other colors also may be had from our distributor in your city. If you do not know his name, or wish further information write direct to us.

THE ROOKWOOD POTTERY COMPANY
Celestial Place, Cincinnati, Ohio

December, 1927

Actual Magazine Ad

Discriminating taste demands impeccable quality in every-
thing pertaining to the table. Rookwood accessories possess
this high quality in infinite variety of color texture and design.

Rookwood may be seen at the exclusive distributor in your
city or we will be glad to have your direct inquiry.

THE ROOKWOOD POTTERY CO.
Celestial Street, Cincinnati, Ohio

ROOKWOOD

October, 1927

For Gifts - ROOKWOOD

As a gift for any occasion Rookwood is a worthy expression of good taste. By reason of the rare beauty of its infinitely varied designs, colors and glazes Rookwood adds distinctive charm to the home.

Rookwood pieces are priced as low as $1.50.
Distributors in 140 cities. We invite direct inquiries.

THE ROOKWOOD POTTERY CO.
Rookwood Place
Cincinnati, Ohio

June, 1926

ROOKWOOD

"If thou hast two loaves of bread, sell one and buy daffodils; for bread nourisheth the body, but daffodils delight the soul." — *Marcus Aurelius.*

Likewise the subtle indescribable satisfaction which comes from the possession of a piece of beautiful pottery, may be illustrated by this ancient and lovely proverb.

Rookwood has an exclusive representative in your locality and we invite your direct inquiries.

THE ROOKWOOD POTTERY COMPANY
Celestial Place, Cincinnati, Ohio

May, 1927

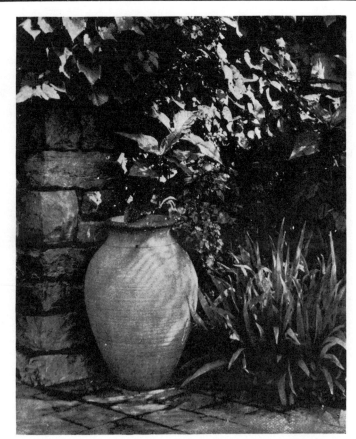

Oil jar made in unglazed buff or blue; or buff with turquoise glaze drip.
Approximate height 26 inches.

R O O K W O O D
TILES AND POTTERY
THE ROOKWOOD POTTERY COMPANY
Mt. Adams, Cincinnati, Ohio

April, 1925

ROOKWOOD

POTTERY AND TILES

Whether old and quaint or ultra and modern
in feeling, tiles possess a charm rarely equaled
by other materials used in home building.

THE ROOKWOOD POTTERY COMPANY
Incline Place, Cincinnati, Ohio

August 15, 1923

Good Art Bridges Time

Roses of Damascus—how remote and romantic, yet how harmonious with modern Rookwood. Ask our exclusive representative in your locality to see our line or write to us direct.

THE ROOKWOOD POTTERY COMPANY
Eden Heights, Cincinnati, Ohio

September, 1927

22

R O O K W O O D

has the vitality of expression which preserves its value through generations. Novelties may come and go, but good pottery will be cherished forever. We have exclusive agents near you, or you may write to us direct.

THE ROOKWOOD POTTERY COMPANY
Mt. Adams, Cincinnati, Ohio

March, 1927

ROOKWOOD FAIENCE

THE interior of the sun room offers many interest-
ing possibilities for the use of Rookwood Faience.
Floors, walls, radiator grilles may be had in tiles of
endless variety as to color, shape and design. Harmony with any scheme is possible.

*Rookwood vases, bowls and other articles of
decorative value also add their touch of
beauty to the room.*

THE ROOKWOOD POTTERY CO., CINCINNATI, OHIO

July, 1919

R O O K W O O D

Like watered silk, are mirrored the surroundings of this lovely black bowl. In its cool green depths, and suggesting a piece of sculptured jade, rests a magnolia motif, supporting sprays of red berries against an amber background.

Rookwood makes bowls in many other forms and colors. You may see them with our exclusive representative in your city, or we invite your direct inquiry.

THE ROOKWOOD POTTERY COMPANY
Celestial Place, Cincinnati, Ohio

June, 1927

R O O K W O O D
POTTERY AND TILES

Rookwood Book Ends and Paper Weights are made in several variations of ship model and figure head design. The Book Ends shown here come in various plain colors and are seven dollars a pair. The Paper Weight is Two Dollars.

THE ROOKWOOD POTTERY COMPANY
Mt. Adams, Cincinnati, Ohio

August, 1925

Design copyrighted

ROOKWOOD

Columbus Caravel Plaque, modeled in five inch relief and having an approximate diameter of 26 inches. An over-mantel decoration, or suitable as an insert elsewhere. Made in colored glazes to meet special requirements.

THE ROOKWOOD POTTERY COMPANY
Rookwood Heights, Cincinnati, Ohio

March, 1924

27

**Actual
Magazine Ad**

May, 1930

THE ~~ ANTELOPE RIDER

The fire of primitive art is given classic serenity
in this rare vase. The forms are simple, vivid,
eternal . . . born of the same art impulse as the
rock-scratchings in pre-historic caves.

The colors themselves are of the wild tropics . . .
old ivory, filched from the shoulders of marching
black men . . . burnt orange, wrung from the flesh
of sun-scorched fruits . . . deep black, dipped
from the midnight waters of the Congo.

Here is a vase you will own throughout the years
with an ever-growing appreciation of its mystic
loveliness. The price is but a hundred dollars.
The height is fourteen inches.

Rookwood pieces of enduring quality
will be found at the following stores:

Tiffany and Co., Jewelers, New York City; Frederick Loeser and Co., Inc. Brooklyn; Kayser and Allman, Philadelphia; Shervee Studios, Inc., Boston; Dulin
and Martin, Washington; Hutzler Brothers, Baltimore; Marshall Field and
Company, Chicago; L. B. King, Detroit; Brock and Co., Los Angeles, Calif.;
Lipman Wolfe and Company, Portland, Oregon. A store of similar quality
represents the pottery exclusively in your city. We invite your direct inquiry.

Rookwood Pottery
Cincinnati

THIS MARK
IS ON EVERY PIECE

THE ETERNAL QUEST
OF POTTERY

The world over, where mountains and rivers combined to form clays, primitive tribes sought to express their art impulses in pottery.

In the days when Kings were in quest of the Nativity, Han potters of China were seeking the realm of fire-fixed beauty. While Columbus sought new geographic worlds, the Sungs and the Mings adventured into still unexplored ceramic fields.

Augustus the Strong of Saxony, questing the glory of synthetic gold, imprisoned Böttger whose liberation was to come with the transmuting of baser metals into the precious; but instead, this old alchemist surprised the more golden secret of porcelain.

This quest in modern times has not been less romantic.

Treking with the adventure in the new world, one finds the vast contributions made by Rookwood to this venerable art of pottery making - - contributions in color, texture and simple forms of good taste, fitting and indispensable in life's surroundings as good pottery always has been, regardless of diversity of period and ever changing style.

Tiffany and Company, Jewelers, New York City; Marshall Field and Company, Chicago; Schervee Studios, Inc. Boston; Frederick and Nelson, Seattle; L. B. King and Company, Detroit; are Rookwood distributors. A store of similar quality represents the pottery exclusively in your city and we invite your direct inquiry.

ROOKWOOD
POTTERY
CINCINNATI

October, 1929

29

The candy box in the group above is priced at $10.00. Filled, it makes a
most desirable gift. The candlestick is $2.50 at any Rookwood dealer's.

R O O K W O O D
the choice gift!

The tobacco jar gives an
impressive note of deco-
rative character to the
man's smoking set. At
$25.00 it is a very ex-
cellent value. The cigar-
ette box is $8.00 in single
color, $10.00 in two tones
The cigarette holder at
$1.50 and the ash tray
at $2.00 complete an at-
tractive combination.

December, 1926

FOR any occasion; Christmas, wedding,
birthday or anniversary, the Rookwood gift carries a certain expression of
personality and good taste that is sure of
appreciation on the part of the recipient.
It adds a note of distinctive beauty to any
home.

Most Rookwood pieces are individual,
each being designed and produced as a
separate composition. The variety of
forms, decorative designs, tones and glazes
allows the widest possible choice in selection.

The pieces illustrated give some idea of the displays that can
be seen at any Rookwood dealer's. Those articles priced
(which are a few of the forms which are duplicated) indicate
the moderate figures at which it is possible to obtain Rookwood.

Rookwood dealers are located in all principal cities. If you
do not know who handles Rookwood in your locality, we
shall be glad to have you write us.

The
Rookwood
Pottery
Co.

Rookwood
Place

Cincinnati,
Ohio

The flat flower
bowl shown above
for a single spray
of wide opening
flowers ranges in
price from $6.00
(8 inch diameter),
to $8.00 (10 inch),
and $12.00 (13
inch).

The cup, saucer
and plate illus-
trate Rookwood
table service in
white with lovely
blue decorative
treatment.

The fan shaped piece above makes an effective
vase for long stemmed flowers. It is priced at $5.00.

Ivory and Jade

Colored pottery pieces, or similar designs
in other color effects, suitable for gifts and
personal acquisitions may be secured
through our exclusive distributor in your
locality at prices ranging from $2.50 to $20.

Rookwood Pottery
Cincinnati

**Actual
Magazine Ad**

April, 1930

ROOKWOOD

Because it is permanent as only beauty is permanent . . . because its significance is more profound than that of most other objects of art, while its cost is small in comparison . . . Rookwood Pottery is the gift superb, the personal acquisition of distinction.

These pieces suggest the wide variety of the Rookwood line. They range in price from ten dollars up. Many Rookwood vases, trays, and other useful or decorative pieces are priced as low as one dollar and a half.

Tiffany and Co., Jewelers, New York City; Frederick Loeser and Co., Inc. Brooklyn; Kayser and Allman, Philadelphia; Shervee Studios, Inc., Boston; Dulin and Martin, Washington; Hutzler Brothers, Baltimore; Marshall Field and Company, Chicago; L. B. King, Detroit; Brock and Co., Los Angeles, Calif.; Lipman Wolfe and Company, Portland, Oregon. A store of similar quality represents the pottery exclusively in your city. We invite your direct inquiry.

Rookwood Pottery
Cincinnati

 THIS MARK
IS ON EVERY PIECE

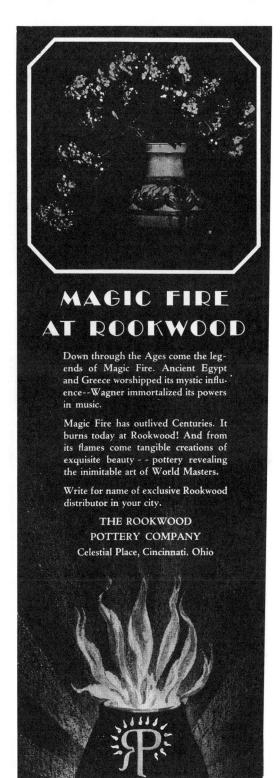

MAGIC FIRE
AT ROOKWOOD

Down through the Ages come the legends of Magic Fire. Ancient Egypt and Greece worshipped its mystic influence--Wagner immortalized its powers in music.

Magic Fire has outlived Centuries. It burns today at Rookwood! And from its flames come tangible creations of exquisite beauty - - pottery revealing the inimitable art of World Masters.

Write for name of exclusive Rookwood distributor in your city.

THE ROOKWOOD
POTTERY COMPANY
Celestial Place, Cincinnati, Ohio

May, 1928

**Actual
Magazine Ad**

November, 1929

The Enduring Charm of Pottery

Beauty bravely conceived and transfixed through fire remains an eternal contribution to Art. Deeply planned or happily fortuitous, such contributions remain suave, calm, impersonal - - venerable creations bridging generation to generation.

Rookwood pieces of enduring quality will be found at the following stores:

Tiffany and Company, Jewelers, New York City; Marshall Field and Company, Chicago; Schervee Studios, Inc. Boston; Frederick and Nelson, Seattle; L. B. King and Company, Detroit; Brock and Company, Los Angeles; C. A. Selzer, Cleveland.

A store of similar quality represents the pottery exclusively in your city. We invite your direct inquiry.

ROOKWOOD
POTTERY
CINCINNATI

ROOKWOOD

Large vase is Oxblood Red, on right Mirror Black vase with Chinese
Teakwood top, vase on left with two handles—Chinese Powder Blue

ADHERENCE to the best traditional standards combined with constant innovations in color, texture and design makes Rookwood preeminent in the field of pottery making.

Rookwood because of its distinctive character and beauty is a most appropriate and expressive gift for wedding, birthday, graduation, anniversary or other occasion. It becomes a rare acquisition to any art collection.

Most Rookwood pieces are individual and are designed and produced as separate compositions. The variety of forms, designs, tones and glazes allows a very wide choice of selection.

The exclusive Rookwood representative in your locality will show you recent samples of Rookwood some priced as low as $2. Direct inquiries are also invited.

Rookwood also produces the finest tiles for architectural uses.

THE ROOKWOOD POTTERY COMPANY
Celestial Place, Cincinnati, Ohio

April, 1927

Below—Rookwood bird bath, oil jar and garden pitcher; made in
plain buff or glazed drip. Bird bath plain or with colored bowl.

ROOKWOOD

35

R O O K W O O D

November, 1927

WHERE discriminating taste is revealed in the fascinating art of flower arrangement, the quality of a bowl or vase is an indispensable factor. Rookwood affords a variety of forms, tones and glazes in infinite combinations of marvelous beauty for table or other decoration.

A gift of Rookwood carries with it the recognition of artistic appreciation. Rookwood pieces are priced as low as $1.50.

Our exclusive representative in your locality will assist you in selecting a piece for your home or for a gift. We invite direct inquiries.

THE ROOKWOOD POTTERY COMPANY
Celestial Place, Cincinnati, Ohio

ROOKWOOD IN THE SPIRIT OF HAN POTTERY

June, 1930

THE Celestial Kingdom was old when the ancient Hans were young. And the green-brown Chinese earth was older still, with years beyond the thought of man. Han artists created pottery - - with form extracted from the inscrutable tradition of an ageless race, with color from the sleeping shoulders of timeworn landscapes.

This vase by Rookwood in terra verte mat glaze with brown black decorations, is as ageless as the earth whence came its clay, as eternal as the art spirit drawn from the dimness of Chinese nativity. The price is forty dollars. The height is about fourteen inches.

Rookwood pieces of enduring quality
will be found at the following stores:

Tiffany and Co., Jewelers, New York City; Frederick Loeser and Co., Inc. Brooklyn; Kayser and Allman, Philadelphia; Shervee Studios, Inc., Boston; Dulin and Martin, Washington; Hutzler Brothers, Baltimore; Marshall Field and Company, Chicago; L. B. King, Detroit; Brock and Co., Los Angeles, Calif.; Lipman Wolfe and Company, Portland, Oregon. A store of similar quality represents the pottery exclusively in your city. We invite your direct inquiry.

Rookwood Pottery
Cincinnati

 THIS MARK
IS ON EVERY PIECE

37

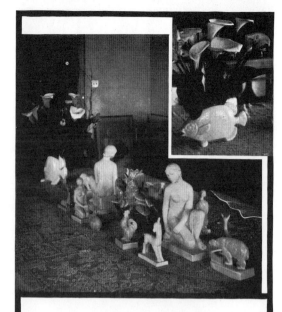

ROOKWOOD'S
SUPREME TEXTURES

In the great art of all time, texture is an important part of perfection. During the best period of Chinese ceramic production, venerable potters were almost unerring in their estimate of its value. Nature, lavish in her manifestation of texture in flowers, fruits, vegetables, animals and insects, offered them inspiration for a goal of high attainment.

Today at Rookwood, texture remains a paramount aim; color and form following in close harmony.

These lovely pieces in Ivory Wax Mat are but one type showing Rookwood's fulfillment of this ideal.

Rookwood pieces of supreme texture
will be found at the following stores:

Tiffany and Company, Jewelers, New York City; B. Altman and Company, New York City; Frederick Loeser and Company, Inc., Brooklyn; Marshall Field and Company, Chicago; Schervee Studios, Inc., Boston; L. B. King and Company, Detroit; Brock and Company, Los Angeles; Dulin and Martin, Washington, D. C.; Frederick and Nelson, Seattle. A store of similar quality represents the pottery exclusively in your city. We invite your direct inquiry.

Rookwood Pottery
Cincinnati

 THIS MARK
IS ON EVERY PIECE

38

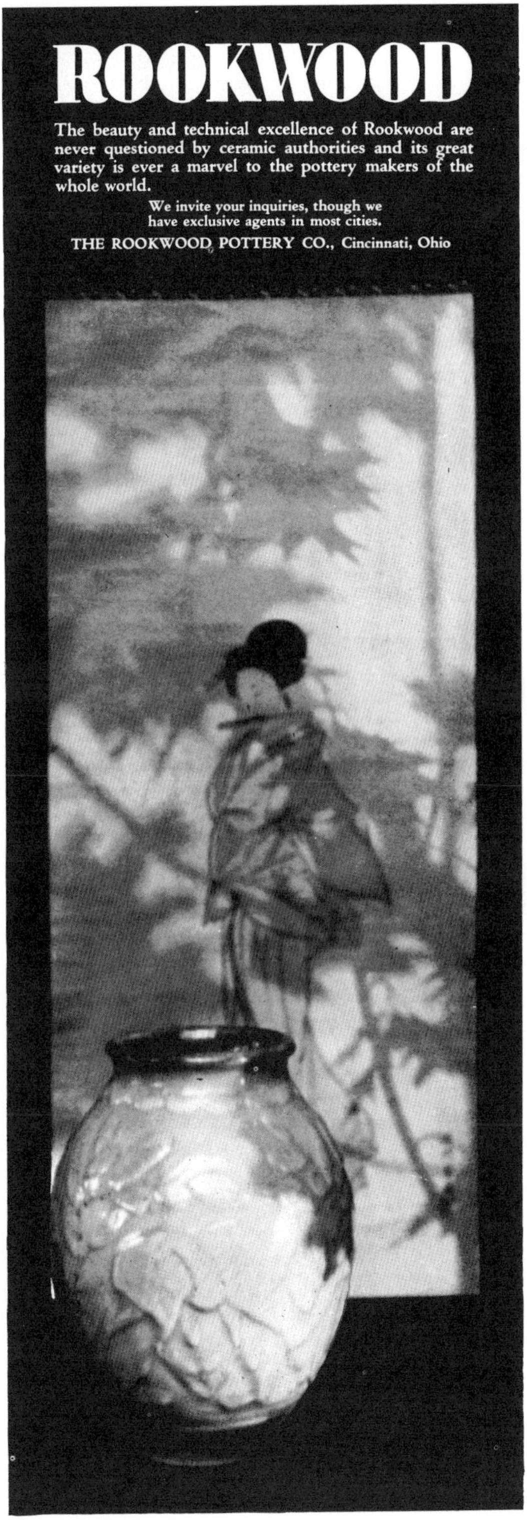

Actual Magazine Ad

November, 1928

Vases

#5145 Scenic vellum vase with birch trees in foreground, lots of autumn colors in leaves. Nice shades of blue and green, 1946, marked with S, special. E.T. Hurley, incised, 9 1/2".

#6614 Hi-glaze porcelain vase, orange and yellow poppies outlined in blue with slender brown stems and green leaves highlighted with brown, white background shades softly to purple around the top, gray and purple around the base, 1936. K. Shirayamadani, 10" h.

Vases

#2005 Covered ginger jar/vase. Decorations of flowers in yellow with dark outlines, green leaves, red berries, brown branches. Wax matt glaze in pink and yellow, 1928. M.H. McDonald, 7 1/2" (both pieces).

#2061   Scenic vellum vase, (scene of brees) in foreground in greens and dark grays, purple mountains in background, in blues, greens and browns, 1920. Signed L. Asbury, 7 3/4".

Left to Right

#901G Iris glaze vase. White carnation decoration, background dark gray at top graduating to lighter gray then white. 1903, Ed Diers, impressed W & S, 9"h.

#2039E Scenic vellum vase. Deep blue and purple trees and background in greens and pale green with yellow in the sky, 1919. L.

Left to Right

#690C Porcelain vase. Small cranberry colored flowers with creamy centers, brown branches connect flowers, cranberry color inside. Light brown bottom then section from bottom to top is creamy background, 1926. Lorinda Epply, 10 1/2" h.

#581E Floral vellum vase. White and pink dogwood decoration with green centers, dark branches. Dark blue top to green to pink background, 1914. Katherine Van Horn, 9 1/2"h.

Vases

Left to Right

#907F Vellum vase, delicate white clover decoration with touches of pink and yellow, pale blue to white background, 1905. A.M. Valentien, 7 1/2".

#2672 Wax matt vase, orange to black at bottom. Six sided, red flowers, dark green leaves. Decoration all outlined in black, 1924. M.H. McDonald, 8".

#2033 Scenic vellum vase. Pale blue trees in a heavy slip with thick deep green grass around bottom. Pale green along tree line, pink in sky. S.E. Coyne, 1914.

Left to Right

#1870 Vellum vase, with decoration of pansy in purple, yellow and white. Background pink to light blue, 1907. C. Steinle, 6".

#S2132 Porcelain vase with red floral decoration on white ground. Brown and green branches, brown centers on some flowers. Hand thrown, original hole for lamp, 1936. Signed on side M.H. McDonald, 12".

#2081 Wax matt vase, blue to pink with deep red flower with yellow center, green leaves, two handles, 1920. L.N. Lincoln, 3 1/2".

Vases

#2463 Floral vellum vase, grey/blues to yellow ground, extensive decoration of pink flowers, small yellow buds and flat green leaves and stems, 1925. Ed Diers, 8".

#6835 Porcelain vase, cylinder shape. Decoration of deer and abstract flowers in dark blue, hi-glaze, peach ground, 1945. E. Barrett, 7".

#942E Carved matt vase. Pale green ground with incised decoration of leaves and vines in deeper green and incised pink flowers in pink, lined in blue, 1905. S.E. Coyne, 5".

#1839 Carved wax matt vase. Deep purple and blue glaze with incised butterflies lined in navy blue with spots of green and two sections of wings with green glaze, 1913. C.S. Todd, 6 1/2".

#400 Covered vase, standard glaze. Decoration of green and yellow dragon surrounded by clouds against a background shading from orange to brown with very light yellow and green highlights which give the appearance of a goldstone glaze. Tail of dragon and clouds painted onto lid, small butterfly handles on either side, red clay body, 1888. K. Shirayamadani, 7"h x 6"w.

43

Vases

Left to Right

#6206F Wax matt vase,decoration of blue, orange, red and purple crocus with green leaves outlined in black, background of green and orange, green interior, 1931. M.H. McDonald, 5" h.

#130 Wax matt vase, blueberry decoration with yellow and orange leaves, outlined in black, bright yellow to green ground with blue-green around top, 1930. L.N. Lincoln, 7" h.

Vases

Left to Right

Iris glaze vase, unusual shape of Oriental influence with small closed neck atop wide shouldered flaring form, delicate decoration of wild roses in white, peach and yellow with green leaves and branches, superbly painted on green to ivory ground. 1908, by CC Lindeman, uncrazed, 6" h.

Iris glaze vase, finely painted poppies swirling around the shouldered vase. White poppies with green stems against the ground of ivory, light green and chocolate brown. Decorated in 1903 by F. Rothenbush, 8"h.

Vases

Bisque vase, light tan background with beautiful painted blue daisy style dec., cream and brown centers, brown and green leaves, a large painted dragonfly, gold highlights, gold band top and bottom with impressed designs, 1883. A.R. Valentien, 10 1/2".

Vases

Silver overlay vase, all over silver in Victorian style, underglaze decoration of flowers. 1897, J. Zettel, 10" h.

#2983 Porcelain vase, huge example with impressionistic
butterfat hi-glaze, deep green to black ground with red,
yellow, blue, orange and green stylized floral decoration,
1930. E.T. Hurley, 15".

Vases

#925C Iris glaze vase, pink and white thistle decoration with light green leaves on a dark grey, purple to pale green ground, 1906. L. Asbury, 10".

Vases

#30D Scenic vellum vase, landscape beautifully painted
in great detail, slender trees in foreground, 1917. Ed
Diers, 10".

Vases

#2918B Butterfat glaze vase with richly colored floral decoration.
Signed and dated 1926 by E.T. Hurley, 12".

Vases

#614B Iris glaze vase. Five large
geese in flight around vase, detail is
incredible, their bodies are fluffy
white feathers with touches of grey,
wings are spread in flight, the yel-
low/orange beaks are open and you
can almost hear them honking,
yellow-orange feet are dangling in
the air, background is dark grey at
top shading to lighter grey to yellow
bottom, 1904. A.R. Valentien (full
script signature) at 14 1/4".

Vases

(2 Views of same vase)

Iris glaze vase, pale green with decorated band at top of dark geese flying into dark swamp land framed by a pink sky, 1911. Decorated by Kataro Shirayama-dani, 7".

Vases

#1846 Porcelain hi-glaze scenic vase. Scene of harbor with sailboats, pinkish-brown around top and bottom, pinkish-brown mountains with blue mountains in distance, water and sky palest green to cream. 1915, Sara Sax, 8 1/2".

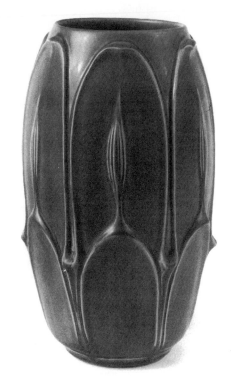

#2492 Vase, finely molded leaves with exceptional definition in Ars and Crafts style. Light green matt glaze, 1920. Designed by William P. McDonald, 12"h x 7"w.

Vase, squeezebag and slip decoration with rendition of flowers arranged in Art Deco style, dark green and blue ground with brown flowers in relief, 1928. Elizabeth Barrett, 18".

#1664C Hi-glaze porcelain vase. Decorated with white and yellow honeysuckle with slender blue leaves, the background is pink to pale blue to darker blue. Banded top and bottom in dark blue, 1922. Decoration by Shirayamadani, 13"h.

Vases

#939C Floral vellum vase, background
shades from pale grey-blue, yellow to
peach, soft and beautiful decoration of
roses in shades of peach, yellow centers,
dark green and brown leaves and
branches, 1907. Fred Rothenbush, 9".

Vases

#463B Vase, with blue and green wax
matt glaze, sharply molded leaf and stylized floral design around bottom, 1915,
20"h x 11"w.

Vases

#734D Iris glaze with an unusual Venetian landscape, Venetian boats with sails, nice cloud work in sky, a small house on stilts in foreground with a man in boat in front, beautiful blue colors with creams, white and brown in the scene, 1900. C. Schmidt, 6 3/4"h.

Vases

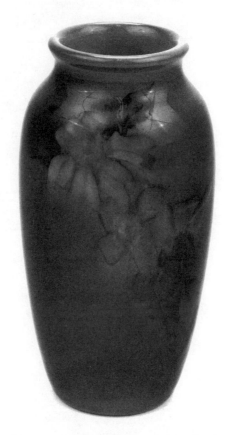

#80B Seagreen vase, deep green back-
ground with white roses centered with
yellow, deep green branches with thorns,
1903. Sally Coyne, 7".

Vases

#2918E Pottery vase, dark orange and brown
wax matt, dec. of llamas and deer in a thick
white glaze, great example of American Art
Deco, 1929. W.E. Hentschel, 7".

Vases

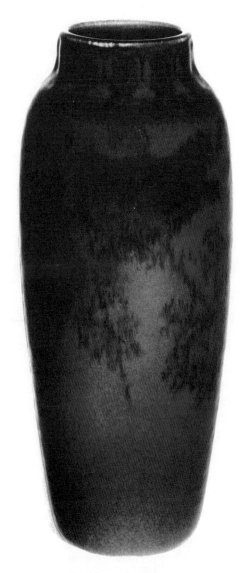

#2313 Porcelain vase. Painting of fluffy bird on branches surrounded by red flowers and green leaves. Dark blue and green floral design around top, deep red background, dark brown inside, 1929. E.T. Hurley, 10"h.

Vases

#815 Iris glaze vase. Large iris flowers in white outlined in dark peach color, leaves are also white and outlined. Very pale peach to creamy yellow background, 1897. A.R. Valentien/W, mark of a cross in a triangle impressed in bottom, 7"h.

Vases

Left to Right

#919E Iris glaze vase, background shades green to white, lavender flowers, green leaves, 1904. L. Van Briggle, 4".

#581D Floral vellum, background shades from green, yellow, pink to deep blue under decoration of blue and white hydrangea, green leaves, 1914. Fred Rothenbush, 8" x 10"h.

#389 Porcelain vase. Mustard yellow to yellow-green ground with red, yellow and brown floral decoration, leaves in shades of green, brown bands bottom, 1925. Lorinda Epply, 4" x 6".

#660 Wax matt vase, yellow and red, green around bottom. Blue inside top, red and yellow flowers outlined in blue, green leaves, brown branches, 1936. K. Shirayamadani, 7".

Vases

#6079 Porcelain vase. Lavender to cream back-
ground, stylized floral decoration in purple, green,
yellow and cream outlined in black, 1930. Artwork by
Sara Sax, 19".

Vases

#907B Standard glaze vase. Detailed brown pinecones and branches with green needles on a dark brown to deep green and yellow background, 1902. M.A. Daly, 17".

#1358 Iris glaze vase. Lavender flowers with yellow and green centers, curving green vines and leaves. Background shades from deep green, pale green, white to lavender top, 1908. C. Schmidt, 13".

Vases

#503 Brown glaze vase. Three handles coming out of top edge and curving to center of vase. Detailed decoration of blue berries and green leaves is around the top edge and on all three handles. Under the handles and around the shoulder are odd shaped openings. Background is brown/ orange to yellow, 1889. H.E. Wilcox, LY in clay bottom, 5 1/ 2"h. x 7 1/2".

Vases

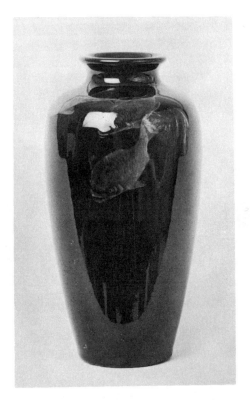

#614F Tiger Eye vase. Dark shiny glaze on red clay body. Orange fish surround vase, excellent detail, 1897. Matt Daly, 6".

#S1454 Brown glaze vase with three handles. Decoration
is a detailed painting of orange poppies all around the vase
with trailing green vines. Dark brown to orange background, 1899. A. B. Sprague, 9 1/2".

Vases

#932C Matt glaze vase with carved pedestal base. Vase is tapered cylindrical form with green to lavender matt glaze. Base of reticulated green leaves entwined with deep lavender flowers, 1904. Signed by K. Shirayamadani, 15".

Vases

Left to Right

#614C Carved matt vase. Dark blue and brown glaze with carved leaf design with red, brown and blue drip, 1914. C.S. Todd, 13".

#935E Carved matt vase. Blue with green matt glaze. Crocus design, 1907. C.A. Duell, 6 1/2".

#1920 Carved matt vase. Chocolate brown with overcast hints of blue, carved raised design of red and green grapes with blue leaves, 1912. Modeled by C.S. Todd, 10".

#1120 Porcelain butter fat glaze vase. Multi-colored geometric and floral design on peach background. Dark brown inside, 1929. Sara Sax, 5" x 5 1/2".

#2721 Porcelain vase, floral design over paisley like background, blue and white, 1924. Sara Sax, 6".

#6628 Wax matt vase. Colorful floral decoration with reds, blues and greens on a background from pink to ivory to green with blue around top, 1937. Executed by K. Shirayamadani, 5" x 5 1/2".

Miscellaneous

#495B Standard glaze pitcher, light clay body & glaze in predominately green/yellow with slight touch of brown, pale yellow/green daffodils touched with brown, slender green and brown leaves, 1890. Marked with S, K., Shirayama-dani, 9".

#456 Cream pitcher, very dark brown glaze to deep reddish/brown with dark orange flowers, crimped top edges. 1903, L.N. Lincoln, 4 1/2" h.

#698 Brown glaze vace with triangular top. Orange, green to dark brown, nice large orange clover dec. with deep green leaves and stems, 1899. K. Hickman, 5 3/4".

#870 Ewer, orange to dark brown background with green, yellow, brown leaves, 1902. C.F. Bonsall, 6 1/4"h.

#412 Bisque ewer, deep peach to pale green ground, detailed decoration of light and dark peach rose, light green leaves with gold highlights, gold highlights on large top and spout, sage clay body, 1888. A.M. Valentien, 9".

Early chocolate pot, limoges style painting in black, green, cream, white with grasses, birds and frogs on a red clay body. Orante handle and spout, 1882. Large anchor mark, signed A.R. Valentien, 9 1/2"h. (No lid)

Miscellaneous

#80B   Red clay body vase. Hi-glaze with heavy rough, gloss drip around top edge. Flowers applied in pale pink heavy slip, dated 1884. Laura Fry, 6".

#45 Basket in Limoges style. Middle is pinched, four feet, background is a chocolate brown on red clay body with white and gold highlights, decoration of black and white birds and black grasses, no artist signature probably ARV or Rettig, 1885, 6"h x 12"w.

#205 Plate/Wall Plaque. Light yellow to brown with reeds and butterfly in dark orange/brown, impressed, 1885. R & a W, signed W. McDonald, 10" diameter.

Miscellaneous

#496C Silver overlay ewer, brown glaze with nice green and brown leaves, silver has flower and ornate vine and swirl design, 1892. Signed AMV/L.

#R840 Silver marked Gorham, ruffled top, 10 1/2" h.

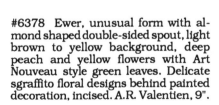

#6378 Ewer, unusual form with almond shaped double-sided spout, light brown to yellow background, deep peach and yellow flowers with Art Nouveau style green leaves. Delicate sgraffito floral designs behind painted decoration, incised. A.R. Valentien, 9".

Miscellaneous

#304 Tiger Eye ewer, red clay body, deep chestnut brown with golden sheeting effect of tiger eye in several places, delicate yellow floral decoration, yellow and dark brown branches, 1886. M.A. Daly, 8 1/4".

#54A Pitcher, ginger clay body, hi-glaze, limoges style decoration of black grasses, blue butterfly, white clouds in background. 1884, Laura Fry, 8"h.

Miscellaneous

Jardiniere, green hi-glaze, touches of black, beautiful detailed painted decoration of yellow flowers, large green leaves and vines, 1887. Matt A. Daly, 13"h x 14" diameter.

Early hi-glaze vase, bottom section has black background with heavy slip decoration of green frog chasing lady bug, black cattails, grasses with gold highlights, tan upper section has cherry blossom tree with peach color panel next to it including artist initials of A.B. Sprague above date February 10, 1882.

Opposite side has white flowers with black leaves and dragonfly against a dark orange panel, small black circle with comical open-mouthed green fish, two other small circles with Oriental designs. Impressed, ginger clay, 8"h x 8"w.

Miscellaneous

Bottle with grey/blue crystalline glaze incised with white decoration, 1951. L. Holtkamp.

#2308 "Chinese plum" vase, purple glaze with white floral decoration, 1927. Signed H.E.W., 7 1/4".

#84 Carved vellum vase. Large lotus flower carved out at top with petals forming edge of vase. The stem arches up as part of the top edge and goes around body of vase to bottom edge. The flower is pale greenish/white with pink on tips of petals, the remainder of the body is a large leaf in soft green with edges folded back at top, 1904. Marked #51CZ, K. Shirayamadani, 5 1/4" diameter x 6 1/2" h.

Miscellaneous

#889C Carved corn matt jug. Deep green matt with touches of brown on corn. Signed by S.E. Coyne, and K. Shirayamadani, 1906. Marked Mizpah Virginny, December 25, 1906, initials on back, 6 1/4"h.

#672 Humidor, brown glaze. Brown bulldog with collar and leash decoration, 1903. E. T. Hurley, 7". Initials LNL on lid.

Miscellaneous

#R353 Jug, silver overlay, decoration of ear of corn, silver is ornately done in leaves and bunches of grapes, stopper covered with silver, inscribed January 7, 1893. E. Abel, 8"h.

#764C Red clay vase with bronze overlay of a bat, unusual example in dark brown/mahogany color, hi-glaze, bronze band around top with bronze bat wrapped over top edge and on vase, 1899. K. Shirayamadani, 5".

Miscellaneous

#688 Standard glaze vase. Detailed and colorful seashells among seagrasses. A 5" wide body tapering to 1 1/2" top, green to light orange ground, 1894. O.G. Reed, 3"h.

Left to Right

#414 Standard glaze cup and saucer. Fluted edge on saucer and cup with finely painted floral decoration of yellow and peach flowers with green leaves, 1889. A.B. Sprague, 6" plate and 3"h cup.

#2504 Sphinx inkwell, brown matt, 1922. No lid, 10"h.

#635 Standard glaze chamberstick with curled handle. Yellow and green clover decoration, 1901. F.V., 3'h.

Limoges style pitcher, thick slip decoration with Oriental person fishing, birds flying in background amongst bamboo, in cream, green, black and white with gold highlights, red clay body, 1882. Maria Longworth Nichols, 10" h.

#T521 Brown glaze ewer. Light yellow/brown to orange to green with leaves, blossom and nuts, artwork in lovely yellow, brown and green, 1890. Marked with S, A.R. Valentien/L, 15 3/4" h.

Miscellaneous

#393 Bisque potpourri jar, blue to pale peach ground, heavy slip decoration of peach and white mums, crimped pie crust top edge, lid has smooth side and pointed side, 1888. Illegible artist signature, 5" h.

84

#830C Standard glaze three handled loving cup. Unusual painted decoration of ghost with bats flying overhead against light green to brown background, band of silver plated bronze overlay forms design of clouds and moon around top. Inscribed in overlay, "St. Louis Harvard Club from Cincinnati Harvard Club", 1899. H.E. Wilcox, 6"w x 7"h.

#6010C Urn, pastel blues, purples in hi-glaze, 2 handles, design in light and dark greens, yellow, purple, brown, design around bottom in same colors, 1928. Sara Sax, 11 3/4".

#277 Bisque potpourri jar. Fluffy black bird on black grasses, reversable top with cut-out leaf and flower design. Light blue to deep red-brown background with yellow clay body, 1886. Painted by A.R. Valentien, 7".

#12A Jug, blue-green to green limoges style painting, white clouds, brown grasses and bird in flight, gold highlights, large piece with ginger clay body, 1884. A.R. Valentien, 8".

Miscellaneous

#6149   Bookends (pottery), blue/green wax matt glaze, 1921.

#2275   Pelican figurine, white matt glaze, with mouth open, 1931. 4" x 6".

#732B   Standard glaze vase, cranes flying in front of stylized clouds against dark brown background. This is not a standard pot combining a sgraffito and slip painted decoration covered by a fine dark glaze. 1899, Kataro Shirayamadani, 10".

Miscellaneous

#2545 Wax matt. White daffodils outlined in blue on dark blue background, 1926. S.E. Coyne, 11".

#942P Jewel porcelain vase. Decorated with pink and white flowers and blue berries. Background is peach to blue, 1919. A. Conant, 4".

#676 Brown glaze jug. Decorated with golden corn on dark brown to orange background, 1897. L. Asbury, 6".

#933D Brown glaze vase. Yellow floral decoration on brown to orange background, 1902. S. Toohey, 7".

#2785 Wax matt vase. Dark brick red mum decoration with light to darker blue background, dark blue top, 1924. E. Barrett, 13 1/2".

#1781 Wax matt vase. White and pink cherry blossoms outlined in blue, with brown branches, blue to pink background, 1929. K. Jones, 6 1/2".

#915C Brown glass vase. Dark orange cherry decoration with green leaves and branches, fruit has a golden color to it, background is orange to brown, 1902. C.C.L., 7"h.

#951E Wax matt vase. Floral decoration, light blue flowers tipped with brown, brown and green leaves. Background is blue/green with touches of darker green at the top to deeper green at bottom, 1929. MH McDonald, 7 1/2".

#839B Wax matt vase. Floral decoration of blue roses outlined in black. Orange inside vase, background is blue and orange with black around top, 1924. K. Jones, 9".

Miscellaneous

#1356D Scenic landscape vellum vase, (night scene). Dark palm trees shades of pink/grey, pale yellow, green grasses, sky with pale pink, 1913. E.T. Hurley, 9".

#2782 Violet/black vase. "Chinese plum" glaze, A violet floral decoration, 1924. H.E. Wilcox, 10".

#2572C Flat bowl with white and pink magnolia flowers on a background of white. Brown on the outside of bowl, 1922. W. E. Hentschel, 1 1/2" x 12 1/4".

#917D Vellum vase decorated with bare trees against snow and pale blue and orange sky. Blue band around top, 1911. K. Shirayamadani, 7".

Miscellaneous

Left to Right

#2545E Aventurine vase. Small dark green flowers and brown leaves. Background is green to brown with yellow, deep blue-green inside, 1923. H.E. Wilcox, 6 1/2".

#6197C Porcelain vase. Abstract and geometric decorations of black, brown, pink and yellow, 1931. Painted by Lorinda Epply, 6" x 8".

#2914 Butter fat glaze vase. Thick white to black line of blue with purple above bottom black section, center decoration of red and blue birds, surrounded by purple and blue flowers, green leaves, 1927. L. Epply, 8 1/2".

#541W Brown glaze pitcher. Brown and yellow thistle and painted leaves., 1890. AR Valentien, 11"h.

#941E Vellum vase decorated with pink and red berries with greenery. Background is grey, green, white to pale pink, 1913. H.M.L., 7".

#2831 Vellum vase decorated with a band of pink cherry bloossoms. Grey-blue to paler blue background with white band around neck, 1926. E.T. Hurley, 5 1/2".

#2032 Scenic landscape vellum vase. Deep blue/grey top and bottom. The landscape is in blues and grees, 1913. F. Rothenbush, 12".

Wax matt vase with blue flowers and orange centers on a pale yellow to blue background, with two decorative handles, 1935. By K. Shirayamadani, 5" x 6 1/2".

#941 Brown glaze vase with yellow daffodil decoration, 1904. Elizabeth Lincoln, 9 1/2".

Miscellaneous

#6310 Blue matt glaze vase. Molded floral design, 1945, 5"h.

#6375 Porcelain hi-glaze vase. Heavy slip decoration of purple and blue berries with green, gray and brown leaves and branches on a white background, 1955. W. Rehm, 5"h.

Left to Right

#6762 Brown hi-glaze vase with sharply molded figures. Mexican scene with people and animals, 1949, 5"h.

#974C Porcelain bowl with wax matt glaze in blue shades, 1918, 2"h x 5"w.

#2556 Green hi-glaze vase, intricately molded floral decoration, 1965. Impressed Rookwood Pottery, Starkville, MS, 9"h.

#6459 White matt vase, molded floral design with bird, 1945, 5"h.

#6870 Orange hi-glaze vase. A molded floral design, 1963. Registered mark in circle, 12"h.

#778 Bud vase, light blue matt, 1945, 10"h.

#6183F Porcelain vase with decoration of blue birds with blue and brown flowers on a white background, 1944. Hi-glaze 5"h.

#6791 Pitcher, sharply molded Grecian figures. Bright green hi-glaze, 1946, 11"h.

#6799 Hi-glaze vase, green. Squiggly lines on the neck, 1944, 6'h.

Miscellaneous

#733C Standard glaze jug with orange corn decoration. Deep brown, green to orange ground, 1900. JES, 9".

#556B Standard glaze vase. Yellow daffodil decoration, ground is dark brown to green, 1900. C.A. Baker, 13".

#927E Standard glaze vase. Orange and yellow fruit decoration, green stems and leaves. Medium brown, yellow to green ground, 1903. L.E. Hanscom, 7".

#232A Standard glaze round box. Yellow and orange dragon painted on lid, red clay body. Dark orange to brown ground with dark yellow highlights, handles from top edge, 1893. Ed Able, 3"h x 6" diameter.

#518E Standard glaze handled vase. Orange and yellow floral decoration, dark green leaves. Dark brown, green to orange ground, 1900. M. Nourse, 9".

Miscellaneous

#6286 Hi-glaze porcelain box. White to pale blue background with four horses sketched in brown around lid, 1946. L. Abel, artist initials unknown, 5"h x 6"w.

#625A Vase, leaf design with pointed edges forming top, bold blue-greens and brown, bright green interior, 1946. Incisted initials H.E., 6"w x 7"h.

#3349 Hi-glaze porcelain covered vase. Decoration of blue berries, orange and brown leaves on a white background with gray striping, dark blue banding top and bottom, 1946. Signed E. Barrett, 7"h x 7"w.

#3200 Hi-glaze porcelain vases (pair). Light blue band of red flowers and gray leaves against white background, 1946. Elizabeth Barrett, 4"h x 5".

#6039 Hi-glaze porcelain bowl. Thick butterfat glaze exterior in brown, gray and white. Interior with pink, blue, brown and cream geometric design. Lorinda Epply, 4'H x 11"w.

#956 Iris glaze bowl, delicate decoration of pink cherry blossoms and gray branches around top on peach to white background, 1906. Lenore Asbury, 2"h x 5"w.

#6204C Hi-glaze porcelain vase. Watercolor style decoration of purple, white and blue swallows, pink, blue and white waterlilies against green, blue, white to gray background, 1946. E.T. Hurley, 7"h x 7".

Miscellaneous

#1652D Vase, carved Arts & Crafts geometric decoration around top, pale lime green matt glaze with reddish-brown highlights around top, 1911, 9"h.

#969E Vase, pale mint green wash over dusty rose at base, geometric Arts & Crafts design around center, 1907, 4"h.

#1298 Vase with a raised poppy decoration in red and green matt, 1913. Designed by K. Shirayamadani, 6"h.

#2862 Vase with light green matt dripping over incised poppies, 1925, 11"h.

#1877 Vase with carved and raised floral design in yellow and green matt, 1908, 3"h x 5".

#1895 Vase decorated with bamboo-like reeds topped with leaves in hues of dark to lighter moss green, 1913, 7"h.

#2379 Vase, pink and green matt over Arts & Crafts leaf decoration, 1917. 9"h.

#214A Vase, pale mint green vellum glaze with streaks of yellow and pink at base, geometric Arts & Crafts design around center, 1907, 5"h x 9"w.

#947 Vase with solid blue matt glaze, raised curvilinear Arts & Crafts decoration encircles center of vase, 1913, 7" diameter.

Miscellaneous

#2886 Bowl, white matt exterior, lined in blue hi-glaze. Leaf design to interior and forming top edge, 1926, 4"h x 6".

#2301E Pair of covered jars. Green and blue butterfat glaze, 1919, 9 1/2".

#2122 Blue matt vase, molded fruit design, 1925, 4 1/2".

#142 Tea jar, red clay body. Stippled surface, splotches of blue and gold over all of body, smooth center band with white, grey and black butterflies in hi-glaze, 1883. Laura Fry, kiln mark, no lid, 8".

#6510 Green hi-glaze vase. Leaf design, 1948, 5".

#2663-#2663A-#2663B   15 pc. tea set. Teapot, cream and sugar, butter fat hi-glaze, elephants foot style mold with excellent floral decoration in panels and almost paisley style decore around top. Colors are cream/yellow background with rust, red, yellow, green and blue in dec., all dated 1924. All are signed L. Epply,

Miscellaneous

#964 Wax matt vase, dark and light blue. Dark blue outlined flowers and green leaves, 1926. Delia Workum, 4" x 5".

#1343 Wax matt vase. Decoration of red and yellow floral with brown leaves and vines. Background robin egg blue and dark blue, 1928. M.H. McDonald, 5 1/2".

#2978 Porcelain double ink stand. Decorated with geometric designs of purple, black, rose, green and brown, 1930. L. Epply, 3" x 7" x 4".

#989D Carved matt. Deep blue on green matt. Geometric design with Indian influence in green and red, 1915. W.E. Heutschel, 8 1/2".

Miscellaneous

Porcelain bowl, handles, beautiful multi-colored glaze with intricate flower decoration, 1928. S. Sax, 3" x 11".

Porcelain bowl, black and burgundy. Black flowers on burgundy setting inside, outside shiny black, 1920. S. Sax, 4".

Left to Right

#822E Iris glaze vase, red poppies, green centers, green stems to bottom, purple to white ground, 1903. R. Fecheimer, 6".

#670C Porcelain vase. Cream ground with floral decoration around bottom, purple and lavender mums, green leaves and brown branches. Two birds are flying above flowers, 1925. Lorinda Epply, 10".

#80E Iris glaze vase, pink, white to pale green ground. White and yellow flowers, pale green leaves and vines, 1899. S. Sax, 7".

Miscellaneous

Left to Right

#957D Floral vellum bowl. Lavender color bottom to turquoise inside. Around the neck is a light orange/brown band and over band are deep purple flowers with white centers, turquoise leaves with white buds, 1920. Fred Rothenbush, 3" x 6 1/4".

#1828 Porcelain vase. lavender with hi-glaze. Cream color band around neck with pink flowers outlined in pink, rose color inside, 1919. Elizabeth McDermott, 4 1/2".

#12 Jug, limoges style. Decorations in browns and creams with black decoration of bamboo, leaves and bats. A.R. Valentien, 1883. G and kiln mark, 6".

Left to Right

#443C Vase, dark brown glaze with cavalier portrait, 1897. A. Van Briggle, 6 3/4".

#711 Puzzle Mug. Painting of a pig's head on side, dark brown's except for snout and forehead which are shades of yellow and stand out. Dark brown to orange background with hi-glaze, small circular openings all around top neck and edge, 1896. Sallie Toohey, 4 3/4".

#913E Iris glaze vase, pale lavender clover decoration with green stems, 1902. Rose Fecheimer, 6".

Vase, stanl decoration of red 7 deep purple raspberries, green and pink leaves, white blossoms with yellow center. Artist signed, 5".

Miscellaneous

Left to Right

#1925 Porcelain vase, hi-glaze over floral decoration of delicate white, yellow and orange blossoms, brown to yellow ground, purple hi-glaze inside with dark band around top, 1925. no artist signature, believed to be the work of K. Shirayamadani, 5".

#589C Vase, decorated with soaring dark birds covered with aventurine or tiger eye glaze, background green to yellow, 1891. A.R. Valentien, impressed W, L in script, 12 1/2".

#61 Honey jug. Decorated with dragonflies – limoges style. Tan ground, orange to yellow painting, black grass, gold highlights, 1882. M. Rettig, kiln mark, anchor mark, 4".

Miscellaneous

#356E Wax matt vase. Decoration of large purple to blue flowers with green and brown leaves against a light and dark background. Brown inside, 1929. W. Rhem, 7"h.

#1109 Carved matt, deep blue to light green, incised band with flowers in purple, and greenery, 1913. C.S. Todd, 2 1/2" x 5 1/2" w.

#941D Floral vellum vase, orange berries, light yellow with deep aqua around top and leaves, 1916. P. Conant, 8 1/2".

#292C Carved matt handled pc., very dark green with black metallic dripping off carved flower and vine dec., orange, blue and yellow flowers, 1915. C.S. Todd, 11".

#20F Brown glaze vase, yellow floral dec., 1902. H. Strafer, 6".

Miscellaneous

#604C Vellum vase, white with grey around top, with grey berries and leaves, decoration of dark pink and orange birds over the grey, pink inside, 1917. Sara Sax, 10 1/2".

#2254E Wax matt vase, yellow and green with floral decoartion and leaves in reds, greens and blues, 1927. Delia Workum, 4 3/4" h x 5 1/4"w.

#2788 Advertising sign, creamy color hi-glaze, square with Rookwood in block letters, ribbon front with "Cincinnati" and ribbon curled design each end, 1957, 4"h x 13 1/2".

Left to Right

Hi-glaze porcelain vase. Decorations of a horse, cat, dog, deer surrounded by flowers and leaves. Light brown over white background with dark rosy brown, 1933. Jens Jensen, marked with S only, 7".

#438 Trivet, painted portrait of a horse's head in brown with a white blaze, in white hi-glaze, dated 1946. Signed "American Liberty" in dark brown, artist signed unknown, 6" square.

#917C Floral vellum vase, blue background shading to a pale green then pink top, lovely single white rose with yellow center, green leaves and stem, 1908. Ed Diers, 8".

Miscellaneous

#481 Bisque ewer, pale blue to pale peach background. White spider mum decoration with green leaves. Highlights of gold on artwork and around top, sage clay, 1889. M.A. Daly, 9 1/2".

#140 Limoges style plate. Background is pink, brown to blue with heavy white overall, touches of black on one edge, black birds and reeds with highlights of gold, 1882. N.J. Hirschfeld, 1 1/2" x 6 1/2".

#519 Cameo glaze vase with two handles. Peach to cream background with white, lavender, green and brown floral decoartion, 1889. A.M. Valentien, artist. Exhibited at The Mint Museum of History in 1979, 5 1/2" x 6".

#21 Bisque box, tan background with incised fern design on body and lid, gold highlights on body, lid and handles. Top has golden knob on lid in shape of a nut, 1882. No artist signature, 4"h x 6 1/2".

#6005C Wax matt vase, pink to blue with blue floral decoration, green and brown leaves, classical shape with two handles curved above top edge, 1928. Sally E. Coyne, 13 1/4".

#508 Cameo glaze candlestick, decorated with white daffodils on light cream to peach background, 1891. Ed Abel, 4" x 6".

#1122B Floral vellum vase, purple to blue around top with black band on top edge, deep pink inside, pink floral decoration around top section with black leaves and branches, striking color contrast, 1918. Sara Sax, 9 1/4".

#98, #7W Cameo glaze cup and saucer, deep peach with white and brown floral decoration, 1887. Underplate signed by S. Toohey. Cup signed by Grace Young, 2 1/2".

Miscellaneous

#6030 Rooster paperweight (pottery) painted in shades of blue, black base, red and yellow on crown and face, 1952. William McDonald mark, 4"w x 5"h.

#6309 Pottery vase, yellow hi-glaze with blue crystal drip inside, 1932, 8".

#2890 Ashtray (pottery), triangle shaped with butterfly, blue matt, 1926, 6" w.

#6243 Zebra Paperweight (pottery), yellow hi-glaze. Louise Abel mark, 4".

#2345 Statue of lady that forms bud vase (pottery). Green hi-glaze, 1948, 11".

#7143 Ashtray (pottery), dark brown metallic glaze, 1957, 1"h x 8"w.

Duck paperweight (pottery). Yellow and green glaze, 1948, 4 1/2".

#2765 Ashtray (pottery), molded frog on side, green and brown, wax matt glaze, 1925, 6 1/2".

#6116 Ship ashtray, with green and pink matt glaze, 1929, 2 1/2" x 6 1/2".

#2510 Bookends of Egyptain female winged figures (pottery), white matt glaze, 1930. Impressed W. McDonald mark, 5 1/2"h x 7"w.

Miscellaneous

Left to Right

#926C Two handled vase, orange poppies with black centers on brown standard glaze, 1901. Elizabeth Lincoln, 9".

Umbrella stand, grey/blue hi-glaze, light brown clay body, heavy slip brown and yellow peony dec., 1882, 23" h.

#583F Standard glaze vase with green and orange floral decoration, 1893. Sally E. Coyne, 5".

#225 Covered box, black pine branches painted on light brown background, 1885. A.M. Bookprinter, 1 1/2" x 4" x 2".

#406S Basket, orange fruits and bamboo shoots on light green standard glaze, slightly rolled top edge, braided handle, 1888. H.E. Wilcox, S for sage clay, L.Y., 5" h x 10" long.

#614B Standard glaze vase with deep blue and cream irises, dark olive leaves, 1903. Lenore Asbury, 14".

#781B Standard glaze vase with yellow flowers and green pad like leaves, 1900. Elizabeth Lincoln, 12".

#777 Pitcher, standard glaze, decorated with daisies, 1902. E.C. Lawrence, 6:.

Miscellaneous

Left to Right

Illustration to The Tale of the Fox and the Turtle with inscription "Lor Br Fox, you dunno wat trubble is". Scalloped dish, light brown with hi-glaze, inner flat portion with illustration. Gilt edge, 1887. Instription under plate "Uncle Remus subj 35, E.P.C." 6 1/2" diameter.

Illustration to The Tale of the Rabbit and the Fox with inscription "You ain't got no calamus root, is you Br Fox?". Scalloped dish, light brown with hi-glaze, inner flat portion has the drawing. Gilt edge, outer bottom stamped with Rookwood mark and dated 1887 with inscription "Uncle Remus tales by EPC", 6 1/2" diameter.

Drawing of a man and a young boy sitting on stools. The inscription reads "I hear Miss Sally callin, you better run yong". Scalloped dish, light brown with hi-glaze, inner flat portion with drawing. Gilt edge, 1885. Inscription under plate is "Uncle Remus set No. 102, P. 25, E.P.C.", 6 1/2" diameter.

Plaques

Scenic vellum plaque, mountain scene of Mt. Rainier in background, white, blue and purple lake, lakes edge and trees in foreground, reflection of mountain, pink, blue and yellow in sky. Signed Fred Rothenbush, dated 1921, 8 1/2" x 11 1/4".

Scenic vellum plaque, landscape with mountain range in bright blue, trees and flat land in soft green and pinkish-brown, sky is blue shading to yellow and pink-brown with same colors reflected in water, titled "A Quiet Stream". M.G. Denzler, 8" x 11".

Plaques

Faience tile, colorful scene with three trees carved and raised from surface in brown with purple, ground in shades of green with incised lines and shadows, incised line of purple and blue trees in background, impressed back Rookwood Faience #1157, C.A. Duell, initialed on front. 7" x 9"h.

Snow scene vellum plaque, unusual colors of green for clouds, pink along tree line, heavy slip decoration of white snow on trees in background and foreground, tall trees in foreground with deep green leaves top, pale lavender highlights, 1915. S.E. Coyne, 9" x 11".

Plaques

"Anchored in the Lagoon, Venice". View of five ships on water, Venetian scene painted by C. Schmidt, 1916, on reverse. plaque is 7 1/2" x 9 1/2".

Harbor scene plaque, vellum glaze. Typical Schmidt colors of blues, several prominent boats in foreground, colorful sails on boats, two with strips in blue and cream, other greens, others pinks and creams, few other boats in distance and shoreline, signed C. Schmidt, plaque is 8 1/2" x 11 1/2".

Plaques

Scene of a boat moored in lagoon with windmills and houses in background, extremely sharp detailed plaque, finely painted . Decorated by Carl Schmidt, excellent color. 9" x 11".

Plaques

Boats with sails on water with life-like reflections, cream to blue sky, sails of grey, green pink and yellow, pottery plaque. Venetian harbor scene painted by Carl Schmidt, c. 1925. plaque is 10"h x 12"w.

Decoration of yellow mums on light green leaves, background is light mottled green to dark green in center, sea green plaque, underglaze very finely pained by A. R. Valentien. This is a plaque, not an architectural piece, signed on front in full signature. Circa 1900, 9" x 13".

Plaques

Evening scene of riverbank with trail to water. Scenic plaque, unusual green vellum glaze, green in sky. Signed E. Diers lower left, 1913, 6" x 8", nicely framed.

Plaques

Lovely scene of trees surrounding small pool of water. Soft blues, grey, green, brown and yellow, pale yellow-pink to blue sky. Signed E. Diers, 1915. Scenic vellum plaque 7" x 9".

Titled "Evening Shore", beautiful artwork of dark blue trees against pale blue and cream background of lake and trees, 1917. L. Epply, 7" x 9", plaque is in a nice original oak frame.

Titled "Winter Twilight" Unusual snow scene with dark blue trees like silhouettes in foreground, line of dark blue trees to grey background, sky in deep pink, scenic vellum plaque 1918. Signed Sally Coyne, 8 1/2" x 11".

Plaques

Titled "Sunlight and Shadow" Scene of road by a stream with large trees bordering road, dark blues, purple, brown, yellow and green, sky pale blue, yellow and aqua. Scenic vellum plaque, signed Fred Rothenbush, date covered. 4 1/2" x 7 1/2".

Landcape decoration along riverbank with mountains in background.
Scenic vellum plaque, 1924. Decoration by Lorinda Epply, 5" x 8".

Plaques

"Dover Castle" harbor scene (plaque). A sailboat with orange sails in the harbor. The water is choppy and blue green. The city on the hillside in background is covered by white fog. Signed by Ed Diers, 6" x 8".

Summer scene of a river bordered by trees in greens and browns, with the pink sunset, 1913. Sara Sax, 6"h x 8".

"A Winter Sunset" scenic vellum (plaque). A snow scene in colors of deep blue in the trees and background. Slender tall and dark trees with winter clouds showing through, line of trees in background. A stream running through the middle of the scene and off right edge of plaque, white on ground and sky with touches of pale pink, 1929. Decorated by Sallie Coyne, 9" x 14".

Plaques

"River Path" scenic vellum plaque. Scene of tall green trees along a river bank with purple mountain range in background.The sky is green at the top which fades to deep pink that reflects in the water, 1920. Painted by Fred Rothenbush, 5" x 10".

Scenic vellum plaque. The scene is a riverbank with three trees prominent in the foreground with their brown leaves spreading out across the top of the plaque, The background has a blue mountain range and bend of river with a blue and white sky, 1913. Sara Sax, 9" x 14".

Plaques

Scenic vellum plaque. The lake with slender trees in foreground, lots of green in the foreground. The lake is blue with purple mountain range, the sky is deep orange, yellow to blue in the background., 1919. Signed L.A. (lower left), 7"w x 9"h.

Scenic vellum plaque with tall pine in foreground. Green/blue forest and snow covered mountains in background. The sky is grey/blue to yellow to orange (Late teens). Signed Sax (lower left), 9"w x 14"h.

Plaques

"Bank of the River" Scenic vellum plaque. Colorful landscape in spring shades with trees lining a stream, (Late teens). By Fred Rothenbush, 6" x 9". (original frame).

Scenic vellum plaque, 1918, by Edward Timothy Hurley, 8 1/2" x 10 1/2".

Vellum harbor scene (plaque). Sailboats with
light pink sails against a very pastel sea and sky.
Gray clouds in sky. Signed in right corner C.
Schmidt, plaque is 6" x 8" high, in fram it is 11"
x 13".

Scenic vellum plaque. Detailed gray trees surrounding pond, brown leaves suggesting autumn, soft blues in pond and sky, 1916. Ed Diers, plaque is 10"h x 12"w, framed it is 13"w x 16"h.

Plaques

"Swans at Twilight" 1915, scenic vellum vase, by Carl Schmidt, 6 1/2" x 9 1/2".

Vases

#2363   Vase, 1922, 2 1/2" x 4 1/4".

#2559   Vase, 1921, 4 ".

#5098   Vase, green panelled, 1930, 4 1/2".

#6214   Vase decorated with Antelope, 1933, 4 1/2".

Vases

"Buffalo Hunter Shoshone",
Pottery vase, portrait of young
Indian brave, 1899. Painted
by O.G. Reed, 10".

Vase (Blue Grapes),
1900, 5 1/4".

#2434 Vase in rust Indian
pattern, 1925, 5 1/2".

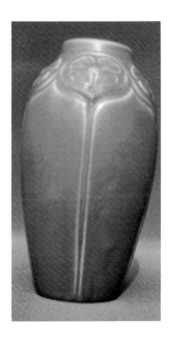

#2403 A & C purple floral
vase, 1921, 7".

Vases

#1907 Vase, 1931, 5 1/4".

#2591 Vase, 1928, 5 1/2".

#2884 Vase, 1930, 6".

#2704 Vase, 1924, 7".

Vases

#6591 Vase, 1938, 4 3/4".

#2088 Vase, 1921, 5 1/2".

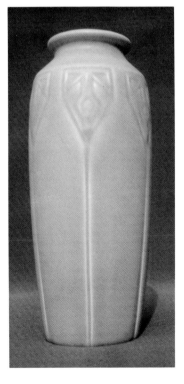

#2393 Vase, 1928, 9".

#2114 Vase, 1930, 6 1/2".

Vases

#2380 Vase, 1930, 6".

#2072 Vase, 1922, 6".

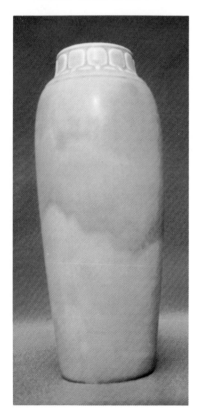

#2318 Vase, 1919, 9".

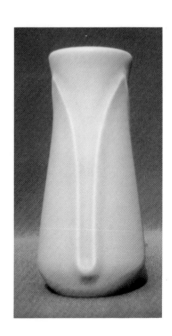

#2091 Vase, 1922, 6 1/2".

Vases

#1342 Vellum vase, 1911. Lenore Asbury, 7"w x 8 1/2"h.

#1902 Vase decoration of peacock feathers, 1927, 5 1/2".

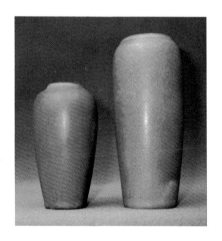

#2179 Vase, green may, 1921, 3 1/2".

#2179 Vase, pink may, 1921, 5 1/2".

#355 Vellum glaze vase, 1912, by Katherine Van Horn.

Vases

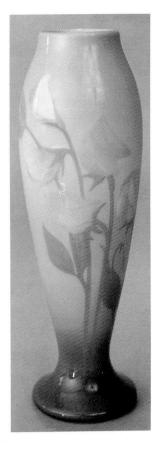

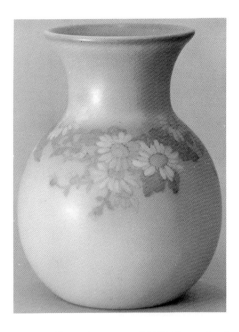

#402 Vellum glaze vase, 1928. Cascade of delicate white daisies and leaves around shoulder, subtle cream to sky blue background. By Lenore Asbury, 6" high.

#949D Iris glaze vase, 1911. Dark to soft green bottom shaded to pink at top with pink rosebuds. 9 1/2" high by Elizabeth Lincoln.

#2100 Vellum glaze vase, 1914. Pink cherry blossoms on brown branches in Japanese style on a gray background. By Edward Diers, 5" high.

Vases

#2759 Porcelain vase, 1924. Band of gold and brown flowers on dark green and gold. By Kataro Shirayamadani, 5 1/2" high.

#1369B Large vellum glaze vase, 1911. White hydrangeas, bluish-pink to purple background. 14 1/2" high, by Lenore Asbury.

Goldstone glaze vase, 1898. Three raised Aztec priests on a brown ground shimmering with gold flecks, 7" high. Artist unknown.

Vases

#357F Jewel porcelain vase, 1920. Pink bleeding heart flowers surround the vase. By Lorinda Epply, 6 1/2" high.

#352E Porcelain vase, 1918. Intricate multicolored paisley design around the upper half of cylindrical vase, 7 1/2" high by Arthur Conant.

#773 High glaze jewel porcelain vase, 1914, by Wilhelmine Rehm, 10".

Vases

#2105 Porcelain vase, 1924. Vines and flowers on an aquamarine background, by Edward Diers.

#271D Vellum glaze vase, 1914. Morning glory flowers shaded from gray to white and green leaves and stems against a cold grey-green to blue ground. 9" high by Carl Schmidt.

#838E Porcelain vase, 1923. A blue iris against a blue ground. 7" high by Carl Schmidt.

Vases

#2437 Vase, 1925, 5 1/2".

#2392 Vase, purple Indian pattern, 1922, 9".

#924 Incised painted matte vase, 1904. Rose Techheimer, 5 1/2".

Vases

Venetian boat scene, vellum vase. Decorated in soft blues, blue/greens, several sailboats against a dusky sky, nicely detailed, touches of purple around bottom, 1921. C. Schmidt, 10".

#952B Vellum vase. Nine swallows flying around top among green vines and leaves. Colors are gray, white and brown, against a gray, peach, to yellow background shading to green at bottom, 1906. Shirayamadani, 13"h.

#922E Scenic vellum vase. Snow scene with vibrant pink color in sky shading to pale yellow then blue surrounded by dark blue trees and tree line with white snow mixed in, 1923. By Sally Coyne, 6".

Vases

#2264E Vase, porcelain, 1925. Kataro Shirayamadani, 5 3/4".

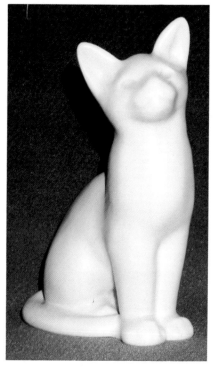

White matt vase, (Cat), 1946. Designed by Louise Abel, 7".

#924 Standard glaze vase, 1901, by Henry Altman, 5 1/2".

Vases

#1848 Butterfat high glaze vase, 1922. By Lorinda Epply, 6".

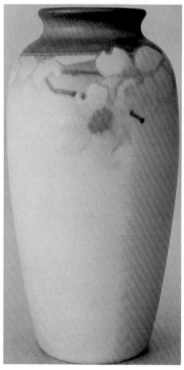

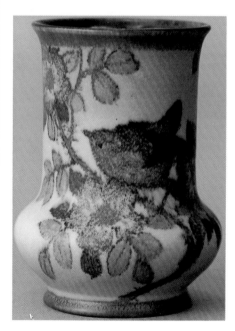

#922D Vellum glaze vase, 1910. Grayish blue background with monochromatic flower wreathed around top. By Lenore Asbury, 7 1/2" high.

#7464S Mat glaze vase, 1933. By Edward Hurley, 6".

Vases

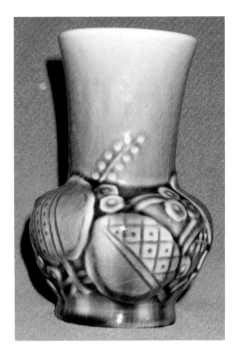

#6363 Vase, 1952, 6"

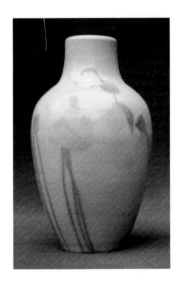

#905E Iris glaze vase. Decoration of poppies, 1901. By Carl Schmidt.

#905F Iris glaze vase, 1904. Irene Bishop, 5 1/2".

Vases

#851D Standard glaze vase, 1901. William Klemm, 9".

#420S Vase (artist 1st year may), 1887. Kataro Shirayamadani, 9".

Vases

#907D High glaze vase, 1922. (Unknown artist), EM, 7 1/2".

#1856B Vellum glaze vase, 1908, by E.T. Hurley. Eight seagulls in flight.

Vases

#922B Vellum glaze vase, 1915. Green vase with three stylized flowers descending in cream and purple from the top edge by Sara Sax.

#913D Mat glaze vase. Olive green background with dark brown raised pods and dark green leaves in art deco style, 1927. By William Hentschel, 8" high.

Vases

#932   Iris glaze vase, 1908, by Lenore Asbury, 9".

#926C Iris glaze vase, 1902. White peonies and green foliage on a cream to bluish gray ground. 8 1/2" high by Sara Sax.

Vases

#459D Standard glaze vase, yellowish orange shrub roses against a brown to orange background, 1892. By Harriet Wilcox, 5 1/2".

#886B Large standard glaze vase, 1889. All over orange mums on a dark olive green to dark brown ground. 13 1/2" high, by Kataro Shirayama-dani.

Vases

#6217 Mat glaze vase, 1932, designed by Wm. Hentschel, 4".

#1062 Mat glaze vase, 1919, 5 1/2".

Vases

#1369D   1928 Mat glaze, 9 1/2"

#6920A High glaze vase, 1949, 19".

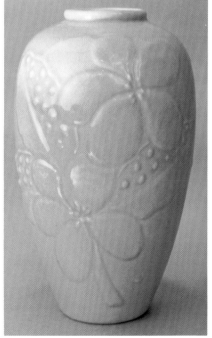

Vases

#804C Standard glaze vase, 1897. Long stemmed gold flowers with long green leaves against shaded yellow to dark brown ground. By Albert R. Valentien, 12 1/2" high.

#807 Standard glaze vase, 1889. Yellow geraniums, green vines and leaves against a golden bottom shaded to dark green top. By Kataro Shirayamadani, 11 1/2" high.

Vases

#1921 Scenic vellum vase, 1912. Kataro Shirayamadani, 7".

#6668 Vase, shepherd and sheep, 1945, 5 1/2".

Vases

#80C Vellum glaze vase, 1930. Pink dogwood blossoms and green foliage against a soft pink background with a black dripping lip. By Lenore Asbury, 7" high.

#703 Vellum glaze vase, 1916. Colorful peacocks among evergreens and other trees in a broad-banded frieze above a dark blue ground. By Sara Sax, 5 1/2" high.

Vases

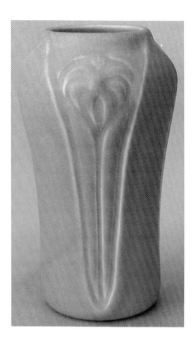

#935 1926 Vase, 7".

#1925 Mat vase, 1915. Bluish pink base color with bleeding blue and red floral decorations around the top; 5 1/2" high by William Hentschel.

Vases

#941D Vellum glaze vase, 1908, 8 1/2".

#6308C Jewel porcelain vase, 1932. Creamy yellow top blending into turquoise body and running areas containing specks of luminosity, 7" high

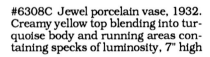

Vases

#946   1915 vellum glaze vase by Lorinda Epply, 10 1/2".

#935c Iris glaze vase, 1903. By Josephine Zetter, 9". On bottom is a paper label of Louisiana Purchase Exposition, St. Louis, 1904.

#932 Carved matt vase, 1910.
By William Hentschell, 9" high.

#6042 Jewel Porcelain vase, 1930. By
Sara Sax, 9" high.

Vases

#1795 Mat vase, 1929, 6".

#942D Vase (green vellum), 1910. By Lizbeth Lincoln, 12".

Vases

#932E 1912 Vellum glaze vase, 8 1/2" by Olga Geneva Reed.

#6350 1946 high glaze blue vase, 4 1/2".
#2977 1945 high glaze brown vase, 7 1/2"

Vases

#328 Standard glaze handled vase, 1887. Yellow shrub rose and buds on a brown background, 6" high. By Kataro Shirayamadani.

(2 Views)

Vases

#512c Standard glaze vase, 1903. By Edward Hurley, 5 1/2".

#58EZ Painted may glaze vase, 1902. Floral design around top. Olga Geneva Reed, 4".

Vases

#534 Iris glaze vase, 1900. Foliage with flower clusters outlined in brown against a cream background, 6 1/2" high, by Rose Fechheimer.

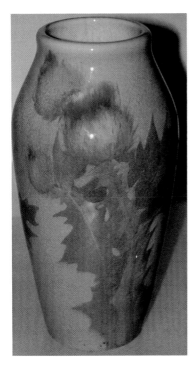

#2905 Iris glaze vase, 1902. By Rose Fechheimer, 8 1/2" high.

161

Vases

#444B Standard glaze vase, 1890. Blueberries and leaves on a golden to dark brown ground. Two small ridged handles on neck of vase, 10 1/2". By Kataro Shirayama-dani.

#S1667 Standard glaze vase with portrait of a springer spaniel on a dark brown background, 1900. By Edward T. Hurley, 7" high.

Vases

Vase, medallion at bottom reads "First Scientific Assembly Cincinnati, Ohio, 1949", 7".

#9260 Iris glaze vase, 1902, by Constance A. Baker.

Vases

#912 Standard glaze vase with silver overlay, 1903. Highly detailed chinese lanterns in reddish orange and dark green foliage against a brown ground. Sterling silver overlay encircles the vase and frames the artwork. By Jeanette Swing, 5 1/2" high.

#732N Standard glaze vase, 1902. Five yellow pansies on long stems hover around shoulder of dark brown vase. By John Dee Wareham, 10 1/2" high.

#S1561 Rare black iris glaze vase, three handled with electroplated silver deposit overlay, 1899. By John Dee Wareham, 8" high.

#139B Rare tiger eye glaze vase, 1884. Under sea life on dark brown ground with shimmering areas of gold striations: "R" for red clay and two museum numbers (52:01 and PO45). 14" high, by Albert R. Valentien.

Vases

#1096 Rare vellum glaze vase, 1923. Red and orange persimmons with green leaves against an even tan ground. Marked with "Yv" for yellow vellum. 5" high, by Lenore Asbury.

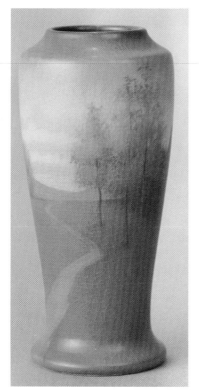

#1356E Vellum glaze vase; medium green bottom with tree line in greens and fall colors. Blue sky with white clouds and gray around top, one cleared area with blue mountain range in background and road spreading wider and dropping off bottom edge of vase, 1914. Decorated by Carl Schmidt, 7 1/4".

Vases

#730 Mat glaze vase, 1925. By Katherine Jones, 6 1/2".

#909C Sea green vase, marked with incised "G", 1900. By Sallie Toohey, 8 1/2" high.

Vases

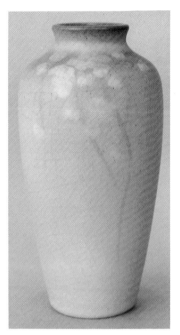

#614F Vellum vase, 1912. By Carolyn Steinle, 6 1/4".

#1358D Black iris glaze vase, 1909. Silhouettes fo trees against a light green shore and sky, 8 1/2" high, by Sallie E. Coyne.

#129 Limoges type vase, black cobwebs and spiders in a maze of brown. Yellow and gold brush strokes, 1882. By the founder of the Rookwood Company, Maria Longworth Nichols, 7" high.

#6112 Mat glaze vase, 1929. Two cows and a nursing calf. 8 1/2" high, by William Hentschel.

Vases

#1927 Vellum glaze vase, 1927. Sky blue with garland of white daisies around the top. By Edward T. Hurley, 4" high.

#614E Vellum glaze vase, 1926. Detailed columbine flowers and leaves in shades of blue and green. By Edward Diers, 8 1/2" high.

Vases

#1654C Vellum glaze vase, 1909. Three birds sitting on a willow tree branch against an aqua blue and cream ground. By Kataro Shirayamadani, 11 1/2" high.

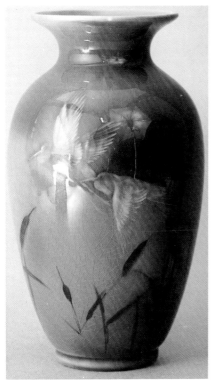

#704 Sea green glaze vase, 1895. Two cut back storks flying above silhouette cattails against a green "G" for sea green designation by Olga Geneva Reed, 8" high.

171

Vases

#942B 1903 mat vase, 12".

#1661 Vellum glaze vase, 1914, by Lorinda Epply, 9" high.

Vases

#560W 1899 Iris glaze by Edward T. Hurley, 9".

#856A Mahogany glaze vase, 1898. "M" artist full signature–Albert Valentien, 17" high.

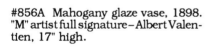

Vases

#991 Vase painted may, 1909. Olga
Geneva Reed, 4 1/2".

#272 Wax may vase, 1931. Lenore
Asbury, 6 1/2".

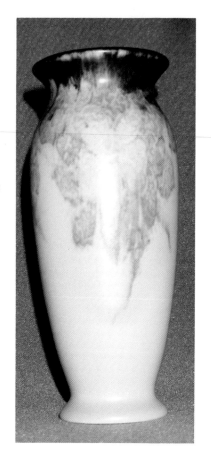

Vases

#6476 Water vase (four pan-
elled) decorated with a frog,
birds, and a fish, 1944, 8".

#1358   Vellum glaze vase, 1925.
Lenore Asbury, 6".

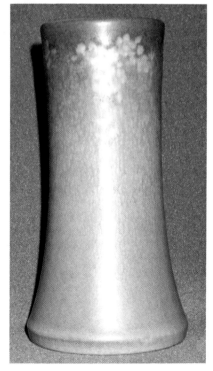

175

Vases

#917A Portrait "After Franz Hals", standard glaze vase, 1903. Deep green to deep brown background. By Grace Young, 12"h.

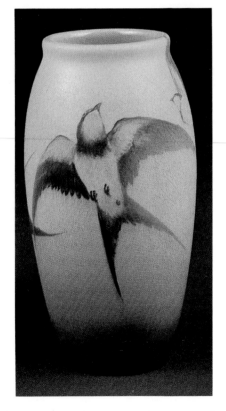

#917B Hi-glaze vase. Three painted swallows soaring around form. Background is brown against dark gold, 1906. C.C. Lindeman, 9".

Vases

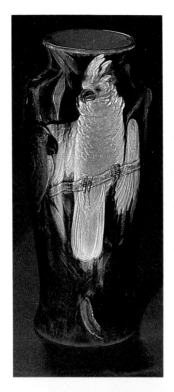

#1664D Porcelain vase, hi-glaze, this type of glaze is quite rare and was produced for a short period of time, refered to as "Japanese Plum", This vase is carved and painted, 1924. Decoration of two cockatoos on a branch, one bird has his wings spread and is white with touches of deep purple and blue, with blue leaves and brown branches, dark rose interior. Artist K. Shirayamadani, 11".

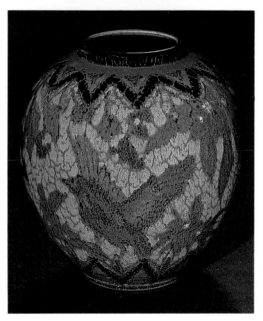

#6204B Porcelain butter fat glaze vase, 50th Anniversary kiln mark, 1930. Raspberry red background with black top and bottom, black inside. Geometric design top and bottom in black and light blue. The center of the vase is decorated with birds and flowers in same red with black and a orange background. E.T. Hurley, 9".

Vases

Crystalline glaze vase, 1937, 4".

Porcelain butterfat glaze vase, 1934, Jens Jensen,
5 1/4".

Vases

#2511 "Oatmeal vase", 1925, 6 1/2".

#356F Porcelain vase, 1925. Kataro Shirayamadani, 5 1/4".

Vases

#2109 Vase, 1917, 5".

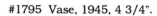

#1795 Vase, 1945, 4 3/4".

Vases

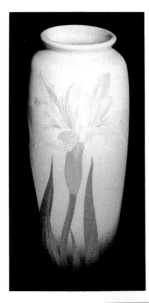

#904C Iris glaze vase. A detailed painting of white irises on front and back with green leaves. Background shades from dark green to lighter green to white and light lavender top. By C. Schmidt, 10".

#S1603C Vase (sea green), 1901. Painted decoration of three ducks in flight in colors of black, grey, green and white on a green to grey background. By M.A. Daly, marked with G, 10".

Vases

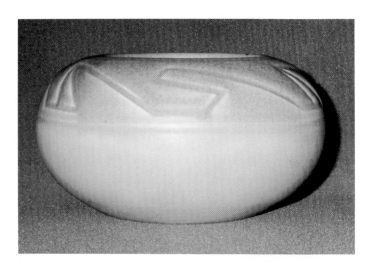

#214B Vase, 1904, green/blue, 3 1/2" x 6 1/2".

#2100 Incised may vase, 1918. Charles S. Todd, 5".

Vases

#6319F Vase, aqua in color, 1932, 3".

#325E Vase (wax may), 7".

#951C Vellum vase with decoration of green and white flowers on a pale green-blue to grey background, 1907. By Fred Rothenbush, 11".

Pottery vase with a painted and carved floral decoration. Green arrowroot leaves are carved and incised, the white flowers with brown centers are also carved and the bottom edge of vase is completed by incised blades of grass. The background fades from a matt brown to brown hi-glaze at top, 1899. K. Shirayama-dani, 4 1/2".

Vases

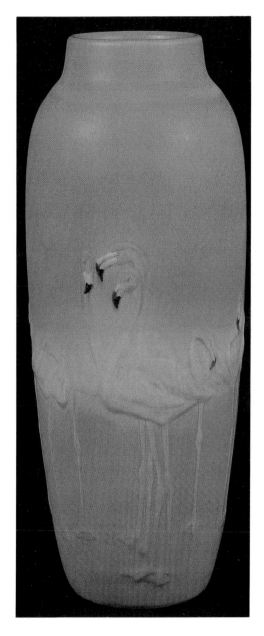

#907C Vellum carved vase, 1904. Thirteen carved flamingos encircle this vase. The flamingos are in blue, white, and pink with black beaks, against a soft blue background. John D. Wareham, 14"h.

Vases

#932C Standard glaze vase, 1903. Mary Nourse, 11 1/2".

#1356E Painted mat vase, 1909. Olga Geneva Reed, 7 1/4".

Vases

#2031 Vase, squeezebag decoration, 1929. Elizabeth Barrett, 5 1/2".

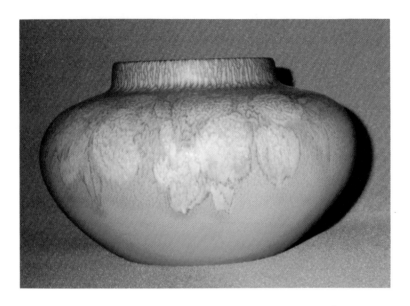

#1929 Vase (wax may), 1923. Herman Moos, 4 1/2".

#935D Iris glaze vase, 1902. Constance A. Baker,
7 1/2".

#604D Standard glaze vase with handles, 1887. Signed
(artist unknown), 6 1/4".

#604D Iris glaze vase, 1903. Josephine Zettel, 9".

#604D Black iris glaze vase, 1906. By Sara
Sax, 6 1/2".

#900B Standard glaze, 1903. Edward T. Hurley, 9 1/2".

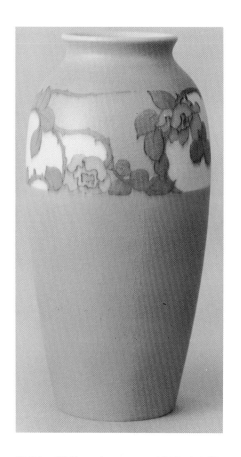

#922c   Vellumglaze vase, 1917, 9 1/2".

Vases

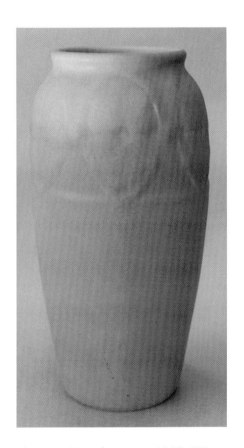

#1710 Mat glaze vase, 1928, 10".

Vases

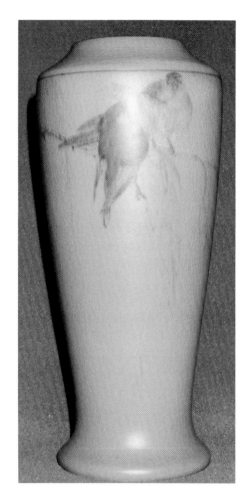

#1356B Vellum glaze, 1918. Charles McLaughlin, 9".

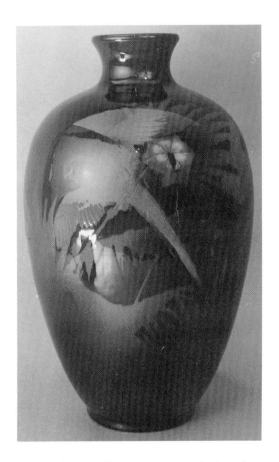

#787C   Rare and important aventurine glaze vase, 1899. Three incised golden parrots amidst golden tropical foliage. The background is light to golden brown. By Kataro Shirayamadani, 11 1/2" high.

#556   Standard glaze vase, 1899. By Kataro
Shirayamadani, 12" high.

#614C Standard glaze vase. Decoration of dandil-
ions at bottom, 1891. Kataro Shirayamadani, 12".

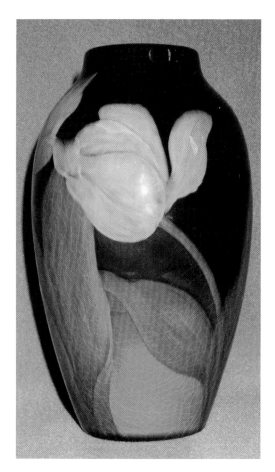

#900C Sea green glaze vase, 1901. Sallie E. Coyne, 8".

Vases

#1655E GV Green vellum vase, decoration
of ships, 1910. Lorinda Epply, 6 1/2".

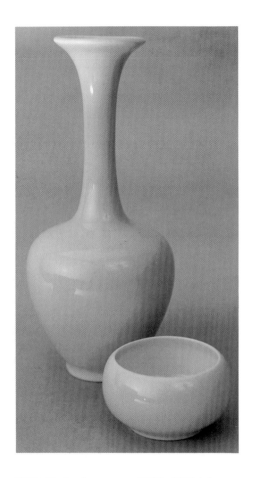

#773 High glaze vase, 1940, 10" high.

#214 High glaze bowl, 1942, 2" x 4".

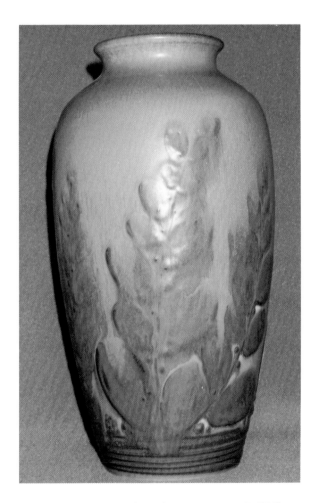

#6140 Vase, squeezebag decoration, 1927. William Henschel, 11".

Vases

#481 Standard glaze vase, floral design, 1893. Kate C. Matchette, 9".

Vases

#S1713 Standard glaze vase, 1902. Matthew
A. Daly, 14 1/2".

Crystaline glaze vase, 1938. Unsigned, 8".

Vellum glaze vase, 1908. By Kataro Shirayama-dani, 9 1/2".

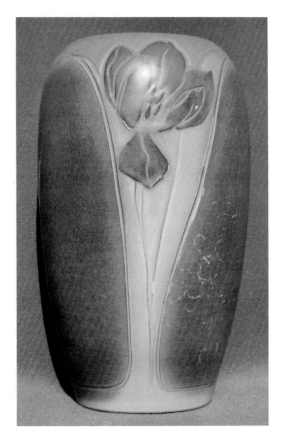

#1126C Carved May vase, 1913. Sara Sax, 10".

Vases

#2984A Porcelain vase with decoration of a white and grey mountain range on a pale blue background. White clouds with grey and brown highlights circling neck. A sailing ship by mountain. The foreground scene is a centaur with bow and arrow being chased by warrior with spear and shield and a deer running beside them, 1948. By Jens Jensen, 16".

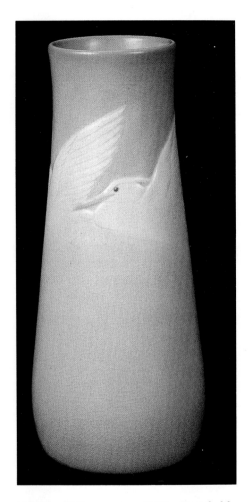

#950C   Vellum vase, 1904. A soft blue
background shading to deeper blue at top,
the color is separated by three carved white
cranes with soft blue on the underside of
their spread wings. They have black eyes
and long grey beaks. By K. Shirayamadani,
9".

Vases

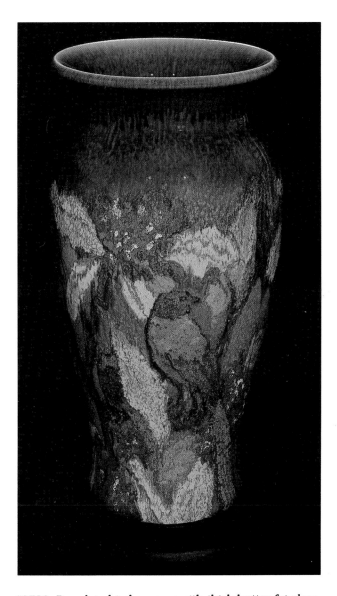

#2786 Porcelain hi-glaze vase with thick butter fat glaze.
Dark blue background with birds and flowers in colors of
green, red, brown and purple, 1924. Signed by E.T. Hurley,
6"w x 11 1/2".

Vases

#85 Pilgrim flask, ginger clay body with bisque finish, incised designs outlined in black over all. Oriental figure in cameo, cupids, lion, palm trees and desert scene. Two small incised designs not outlined of seated rabbit figures. A small dark metal and cork stopper in top, 1884. Unsigned but obviously Cranch, 5"w x 8"h.

#52 Pilgrim flask, ginger clay body with bisque finish. On one side with incised design of three men running in front of brick fence with dog-faced man watching them. Other side with incised design of three men in bowl, inscription reads "three wise men of Gotham went to sea in a bowl", 1884. A small dark metal and cork stopper in top. Cranch, incised and painted, 5"w x 8"h.

#216 Tiger eye vase with a large yellow daffodil decoration with slender yellow and green leaves on a dark orange to brown background with tiger eye around fluted top edge. Red clay body, 1888. Shirayamadani, 13"h.

#904D "After Franz Hals" standard glaze vase. A portrait of a cavalier, in dark browns and yellow against dark brown to orange background, 1903. Grace Young, 8"h.

#218A "Irene Wilike" standard glaze vase. Decoration is of a full figure nude with fabric loosely draped from her waist. The background is a forest setting. Sturgis Laurence, 12"h.

Vases

#560A Standard glaze vase. Decorated with orange and yellow roses. The stems and leaves are shades of green and brown. The background is shades from yellow, orange, brown and green, 1890. M.A. Daly, 16"h.

#905C Iris glaze vase. Large white and grey open iris and buds with green to brown leaves. The background is dark brown, green, white to pale lavender, 1907. Carl Schmidt, 10"h.

#139A Standard glaze vase. Decoration of orchids in yellow and brown with streaks of green, long slender leaves and buds in same color. The background is in shades of brown, yellow, orange, and green. Solid light yellow inside, 1890. A.R. Valentien, 20".

#856C "Wanstall Arwapaho" standard glaze vase. Portrait of Indian brave with single feather against a background of orange-green to brown around top, 1900. Sturgis Laurence, 13"h.

Vases

#741C Aerial blue vase. Scene of cattle moving through forest trailed by a man, outline of village in background, bare tree branches in foreground. Large trees with thick leaves along the path, softly painted impressionistic painting of trees and grass continue around the vase. Completely painted in shades of blue with white and cream highlights and shading in background, 1894. Signed W.P. McDonald, with old paper label on side, red museum numbers on the bottom, 5 1/2"h.

Iris glaze vase, with banded decoration of brown peacock feathers centered with vivid orange and light and dark blue eyes against a background of pale blue-green and thick orange design. Body background in deep blue-green shading to white, 1908. Carl Schmidt, 10"h.

#860 Iris glaze vase with painted slip decoration of two fish in swirling waves. Grey-brown to cream colors with light blue around top, 1899. E.T. Hurley, red museum numbers 386:06, 6"h.

Vases

#800C Scenic vellum vase, groups of brown and yellow trees with orange highlights with green and brown ground. Blue lake and brighter blue mountain range in rear, sky shading from yellow, pale blue to brown around top. Lenore Asbury, 9"h.

#989D vellum vase with three large brown and green fish swimming around shoulder with hint of white waves, against a peach background shading to green top and bottom, light peach color around bottom edge, 1905. E. T. Hurley, 8"h.

#1121C Scenic vellum vase with birch trees in foreground with painted slip decoration of leaves in greens and browns, lake in background with purple treeline, sky shading from deep pink, green to dark blue around top, purple treeline and pink sky reflected in water, 1917. E.T. Hurley, 10"h.

#1655 Harbor scene vase in green vellum glaze. Scene of sailboats and rowboats in harbor with lighthouse and hills in background with colors of dark brown, yellow, green to lighter brown colors, 1904. Sara Sax, 8"h.

Vases

£743C Iris glaze bud vase. Decorated with white and yellow apple blossoms with gray branches wrapped around shoulder, background shades are from dark gray to pale lavender and light yellow, 1908. Katherine Van Horn, 7"h.

#952F Scenic vellum vase, Dark grey-blue trees blending into same color band around top. Light green to blue ground with lavender and pink background, 1913. Sallie Coyne, 7"h.

#614D Carved iris glaze vase. Carved roses around top lightly painted in yellow and pale peach, leaves, stems and background in pale green-yellow shading to white, stems with thorns extend to bottom, 1900. Wm. P. McDonald, 10"h.

#745C Iris glaze vase with pink roses and greenery against a pale green to dark brown-green top, 1902. Ed Diers, 6"h.

#939D Scenic vellum, dark blue and gray trees in foreground, background is dark brown, green to blue with purple treeline, pink and yellow in sky, 1914. Mary Grace Denzler, 7"h.

#952F Floral vellum vase, Band of pink poppies against a white to pink background with long green stems to bottom separating panels of light green, 1909. Elizabeth Lincoln, 6"h.

Vases

#817 Sea green vase, Decorated with four yellow butterflies around white, brown to dark green flowers and grass, dark gray to green background, interesting shaped bulbous top twists to square base, 1896. Lenore Asbury, incised, 8"h.

#A5 Tiger eye vase, with decoration of brown and green crayfish surrounded by yellow and brown grasses against a very dark brown background with light sheeting of tiger eye. Red clay body, 1894. A.R. Valentien, 6"h.

#810 "Apache" (name of Indian not legible). Standard glaze three-handled loving cup. Portrait of an Indian brave. The background is light green brown to dark orange, raised design of feathers and beading on necklace hanging in two sections behind portrait. Silver overlay band at top with Indian designs and birds, silver-plated bronze plaque on one side for initials, unused, 1898. Red museum numbers 329:06, old paper label, Grace Young, 5" x 7"h.

#1658E Green aventurine glaze vase with decoration of a fish swimming around upper section of piece. Deep blue-green around top, sparkling lighter green glaze in sheets like tiger eye, 1911. Sallie Coyne, 9"h.

Bowls

#228E Bowl, 1886, by Grace M. Young, 1" x 4", standard glaze.

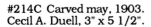

#214C Carved may, 1903. Cecil A. Duell, 3" x 5 1/2".

#211 Standard glaze covered bowl, 1885. Painted and sketch-like flowers on a golden mustard background. 4" high, by Laura Fry.

Bowls

#214E Standard glaze bowl, 1904. Olive green with lighter green leaves and cream colored flowers. 2 1/4" high by Irene Bishop.

#955 Vellum glaze bowl, 1908. Creamy gray with a strand of stems, leaves and pink blossoms. 2 1/2" high by Edith Noonan.

#957B Mat bowl, 1921. Mustard yellow with purple flowers, by Charles Todd, 3 1/2" high.

Bowls

#2152 Bowl, lavender, 1929, 2"h x 4 1/2".

Fluted bowl, 1893. Design of fox and hound chase scene. Some twenty dogs are encircling the bowl, bounding up hill and jumping a fence, three sections show dogs chasing the prey with the fourth depicting the fox entering its hiding place.

Bowls

#2178B 1926 bowl, 14" diameter.

1919 Matt glaze bowl by Arthur Conant, 3" x 5 3/4".

Bookends

#2732 Bookends, 1923, designed by Wm. McDonald, 6 3/4".

Bookends

#2364 1924 Bookends
by William McDonald,
5 1/2"

#2510 1920 book-
ends by William
McDonald, 5 1/2"
high.

Bookends

#2836 Flower bookends, 1946.
By Elizabeth Barrett, 3 1/2"

Very rare lustre glaze book-
ends, 1915. By William
McDonald, 5 1/2".

Bookends

#6252 Bookends (Colonial woman), 1934, 6 1/2"

#6014 Bookends (Horses head designed by McDonald), 1955, 6 1/2".

Bookends

#6124 Elephant bookends, 1957, 7 1/8".

#2554 Bookends (Yellow panthers), 1922, 5 1/2".

Bookends

#2678 Bear bookends, 1934. 4" tall.

#2998 Dog bookends, 1937, 4 3/4".

Bookends

#2655 1935 Owl bookends, 5 3/4".

#2653 1924 Bookends, 5 1/2".

Bookends

#2274 Bookends, 1921, by Wm. McDonald, 7".

Bookends

#6023 Trees, 1929. Yellow and green mat, 5 1/2"
high, by Wm. McDonald.

Bookends

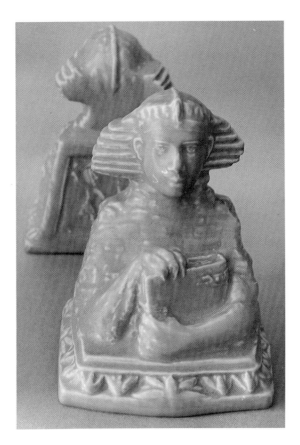

#2503 Sphinx bookends, 1921. Mat glaze, 7" high.

Lamps

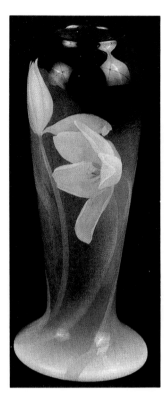

#598 Iris glaze lamp base. White tulips, yellow centers, and large green leaves. Colors of dark grey at top shading to brilliant deep lavender/blue, white around bottom, 1903. Sara Sax, 13 1/2"h.

#614 Lamp base, 1937. Ceramic Portion, 14".

#722 Kerosene Lamp, 1894. By Kataro Shirayamadani, 10 1/8" original brass fittings.

Lamps

Lamp with original factory fittings, 1937. Ceramic portion is 10".

Tea Tiles

#1378 Tea Tile, 1917. A ship with sails, 5 3/4".

#3205 Tea tile, 1925. Castle, 5 3/4".

#3069 Tea tile, 1930. Decoration of a woman with an umbrella.

#3203 Tea tile, 1923. Dutch scene, 5 3/4".

Tea Tiles

#3077 Tea tile, 1929. Parrot, 5 3/4".

#3301 Tea tile, 1924. Duck, 5 3/4".

#3124 Tea tile, 1928. Dove, 5 3/4".

#3207 Tea tile, 1926. Three geese.

Tea Tiles

#1263 Tea tile, 1919. Decorated with apples, 5 1/2" x 5 1/2"

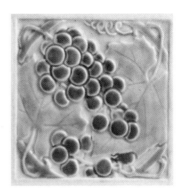

#1633 Tea tile, 1930. Decoration of grapes, 5 3/4".

#3206 Tea tile, 1930. Decoration of a flower basket.

#1631 Tea tile, 1919. Decorated with flowers, 5 3/4".

Tea Tiles

#1794 Tea tile, 1925. Black bird, 5 3/4".

#2043 Tea tile, 1925. Parrot, 5 3/4".

#2047 Tea tile, 1924. Bird with wings spread, 6" x 6".

Tea Tiles

Tea tile, 1900, Faience. 12" x 12".

Miscellaneous

Beer Tankard (two views) 1881-2. Bisque raised ribbon
mark. Cincinnati Cooperage Co., 5 1/2" x 7 1/2".

Miscellaneous

#7133 Spoonrest, 1950, 3 1/4".

#7206 Ashtray, 1937, 5".

#2565 Pin tray, 1931. Owl, mat glaze, by William McDonald, 5 3/4".

Miscellaneous

Powder Box, wax may, 1922.
Lorinda Epply, 6".

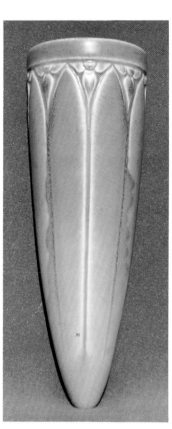

#2107 Wall pocket, 1922,10".

#6820 Plate, 1946, 9 3/4".

Miscellaneous

#838F Pitcher, iris glaze, 1901. Sara Sax, 5 1/4".

#1420 Ginger jar, early limoges glaze, floral design, 1885. Mathew A. Daly, 4 1/2".

#547 Teapot, 1923, 3 1/2"

Miscellaneous

1890's Pitcher, by Shirayamadani, with silver mount lip and handle, 6".

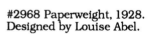

#2968 Paperweight, 1928. Designed by Louise Abel.

Miscellaneous

#343 High glaze water pitcher with two clusters of flowers and small leaves on a light pink to powder blue ground, 1888. 7" high by Mathew A. Daly.

#T1261 Sea green plaque, 1902. A violent sea and sky in greens and bluish greens. 18" diameter by Joseph Jefferson. A paper label of the Louisiana Purchase Exposition, St. Louis, 1904.

Miscellaneous

#479 Jewel porcelain scent jar. Stencil-like yellow flowers and leafy vines on an olive green background, 1921. By Arthur Conant, 6" high.

#1071 Vellum glaze mug, 1910. Soft gray-green with a goose in flight descending into a marsh, 6" high. By Kataro Shirayamadani.

Miscellaneous

#101C Claret jug, 1886. By Anna Bookprinter, 8 1/2". Dull finish glaze.

Paperweight (Bird), 1946, 3 3/4".

Miscellaneous

#772   Chocolate pot, standard g;aze. 1895. Rose Fechheimer, 9".

#772   Covered chocolate pot, 1903. Iris glaze, 10", by Rose Fechheimer.

Miscellaneous

Two views

#1171 Owl mug, 1905. Mat glaze, 5 1/2".

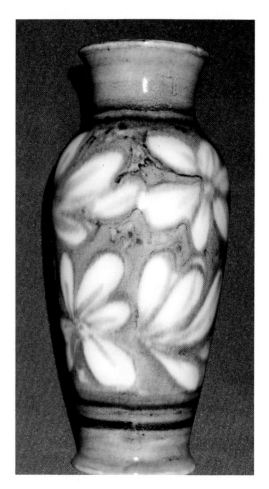

#5855 Porcelain Vase, 1945.
By Jens Jensen, 9"

Miscellaneous

#E12 1963 Mug, 7 1/4", high glaze.

#2336 "P" 1918, 6 1/2".

Miscellaneous

Candlestick, carved vellum, 1909. Unknown artist (illegible name), 8".

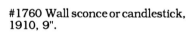

#1760 Wall sconce or candlestick, 1910, 9".

252

Jardiniere, with limoges style background. Painted brown birds flying against background of mottled bright blue, brown, gold, green with white clouds on a terra cotta background, 1884. Attributed to Matt Daly, 11" x 15" diameter.

Price Guide

All items priced in this guide are for items in very good condition. Pieces that are stained, with holes or cracked are worth much less. Items in mint condition are worth much more.

Dealers will not pay collector prices so you must figure 40-50% off list price if selling to dealer.

Remember, this is only a guide. L-W Books nor the author assumes no liability because of loss or gain in using these prices. Items may vary from area to area, so keep in mind this is only a guide.

Page 40
#6614 – $1500-2000
#5145 – $1250-1750

Page 41
#2005 – $500-700
#2061 – $600-800
#901G – $750-1000
#2039E – $500-700
#690C – $500-750
#581E – $300-500

Page 42
#907F – $300-400
#2672 – $350-450
#2033 – $600-800
#1870 – $400-550
#S2132 – $600-800
#2081 – $300-400

Page 43
#2463 – $700-900
#6835 – $800-1000
#942E – $400-600
#1839 – $500-750
#400 – $2500-3500

Page 44
#6206F – $400-600
#130 – $500-700

Page 45
$900-1200
$1200-1700

Page 46
$1250-2000

Page 47
$3000-4000

Page 48
#2983 – $1500-2000

Page 49
#925C – $1500-2000

Page 50
#30D – $2500-3000

Page 51
#2918B – $1500-2000

Page 52
#614B – $15,000-20,000

Page 53
$2000-3000

Page 54
#1846 – $800-1100
#2492 – $500-750

Page 55
$1500-2500

Page 56
#1664 – $3000-4000

Page 57
#939C – $600-800

Page 58
#463B – $1700-2200

Page 59
#734D – $3500-4000

Page 60
#80B – $1500-2000

Page 61
#2918E – $750-1000

Page 62
#2313 – $1500-2500

Page 63
#815 – $1000-1500

Page 64
#919E – $400-600
#581D – $1000-1500
#389 – 500-700
#660 – $800-1200

Page 65
#6079 – $3000-4000

Page 66
#907B – $2000-3000

Page 67
#1358 – $3000-3500

Page 68
#503 – $1500-2000

Page 69
#614F – $2000-3000

Page 70
#S1454 – $1100-1400

Page 71
#932C – $2500-3500

Page 72
#614C – $600-800
#935E – $250-350
#1920 – $400-600
#1120 – $300-500
#2721 – $300-400
#6628 – $500-700

Page 73
#495B – $400-600
#456 – $150-200
#698 – $250-300
#870 – $300-350
#412 – $1000-1500
$200-300

254

Page 74
#80B – $700-900
#45 – $800-1200
#205 – $200-300

Page 75
#496C – $1500-2000
#R840 – $1500-2000
#6378 – $800-1100

Page 76
#304 – $500-750
#54A – $300-400

Page 77
$2500-3500
$1500-2000

Page 78
$300-400
#2308 – $600-800
#84 – $3000-5000

Page 79
#889C – $500-750
#672 – $1000-1500

Page 80
#R353 – $3000-4000
#764C – $2000-3000

Page 81
#688 – $200
#414 – $200-300
#2504 – $250-350
#635 – $200-300

Page 82
$1500-2500

Page 83
#T521 – $2000-3000

Page 84
#393 – $600-800

Page 85
#830C – $2500-3500

Page 86
#6010C – $750-1500

Page 87
#277 – $1000-1500

Page 88
#12A – $1100-1500

Page 89
#6149 – $100-150
#2275 – $200-250
#732B – $2000-3000

Page 90
#2545 – $350-450
#942P – $350-450
#676 – $400-600
#933D – $300-500
#2785 – $600-800
#1781 – $250-350
#915C – $300-400
#951E – $400-600
#839B – $300-500

Page 91
#1356D – $700-850
#2782 – $400-600
#2572C – $400-600
#917D – $600-800

Page 92
#2545E – $500-700
#6197C – $400-600
#2914 – $800-1100
#541W – $1000-1500
#941E – $300-400
#2831 – $350-550
#2032 – $500-750
$400-550
#941 – $400-550

Page 93
#6310 – $60-80
#6375 – $150-200
#6762 – $50-70
#974C – $40-60
#2556 – $100-150
#6459 – $50-70
#6870 – $150-200
#778 – $80-110
#6183F – $100-200
#6791 – $70-90
#6799 – $60-80

Page 94
#733C – $500-700
#556B – $600-800
#927E – $500-750
#232A – $300-500
#518E – $500-700

Page 95
#6286 – $400-600
#625A – $200-300
#3349 – $500-700

#3200 – $500-700
#6039 – $500-700
#956 – $300-400
#6204C – $1000-1500

Page 96
#1652 – $250-350
#969E – $150-200
#1298 – $300-400
#2862 – $300-400
#1877 – $200-300
#1895 – $200-250
#2379 – $300-500
#214A – $200-300
#947 – $200-300

Page 97
#2886 – $50-70
#2301E – $200-300
#2122 – $50-70
#142 – $500-700
#6510 – $50-70

Page 98
#2663-2663A-2663B –
  $1000-2000

Page 99
#964 – $200-250
#1343 – $225-275
#2978 – $400-600
#989D – $300-400

Page 100
$500-700
$400-600
#822E – $450-600
#670C – $800-1100
#80E – $550-700

Page 101
#957D – $200-300
#1828 – $200-300
#12 – $700-1000
#443C – $1000-1500
#711 – $750-1250
#913E – $400-500
$75-125

Page 102
#1925 – $300-500
#589C – $800-1100
#61 – $300-500

Page 103
#356E – $500-700
#1109 – $150-200
#941D – $400-600
#292C – $400-650
#20F – $300-400

Page 104
#604C – $700-1000
#2254E – $300-400
#2788 – $750-1000
$1000-12500
#438 – $400-600
#917C – $500-700

Page 105
#481 – $1000-1500
#140 – $400-600
#519 – $800-1100
#21 – $400-600
#6005C – $50-100
#508 – $400-500
#1122B – $750-1000
#98 & #7W – $250-350

Page 106
#6030 – $200-300
#6309 – $100-150
#2890 – $75-100
#6243 – $150-250
#2345 – $100-150
#7143 – $30-50
$150-200
#2765 – $100-150
#6116 – $150-250
#2510 – $300-400

Page 107
#926C – $500-650
$500-750
#583F – $250-350
#225 – $200-300
#406S – $900-1100
#614B – $600-800
#781B – $300-400
#777 – $250-350

Page 108
$400-600
$400-600
$400-600

Page 109
$2000-3000
$1200-1700

Page 110
$2000-2500
$2750-3500

Page 111
$2000-2500
$1000-1500

Page 112
$3000-4000

Page 113
$5000-7000

Page 114
$1500-2500

Page 115
$2000-2500

Page 116
$2000-2500

Page 117
$2500-3500

Page 118
$2750-3500

Page 119
$1000-1500

Page 120
$2250-2750

Page 121
$2000-3000
$1500-2000
$4000-5000

Page 122
$2000-2500
$2750-3500

Page 123
$1500-2000
$2500-3500

Page 124
$2000-2500
$4250

Page 125
$3000-3500

Page 126
$3500-4500

Page 127
$6000

Page 128
#2363 – $50
#2559 – $60
#5098 – $75
#6214 – $115

Page 129
$5000-7500
$425
#2434 – $95
#2403 – $100

Page 130
#1907 – $150
#2591 – $85
#2884 – $75
#2704 – $185

Page 131
#6591 – $55
#2088 – $50
#2393 – $175
#2114 – $85

Page 132
#2380 – $150
#2072 – $185
#2318 – $80
#2091 – $85

Page 133
#1342 – $1750
#1902 – $125
#2179 (green) – $60
#2179 (pink) – $90
#355 – $600

Page 134
#949D – $2600
#402 – $1250
#2100 - $575

Page 135
#2759 – $2000
#1369B – $3500
$2400

Page 136
#357F – $950
#352E – $1950
#773 – $500

Page 137
#2105 – $1200
#838E – $1500
#271D – $4000

Page 138
#2437 – $75
#2392 – $115
#924 – $1750

Page 139
$1500-2500
#952B – $6000-8000
#922E – $1000-1250

Page 140
#2264E – $2750
$225
#924 – $400

Page 141
#1848 – $800
#922D – $450
#7464S – $2500

Page 142
#63636 – $50
#905E – $950
#905F – $750

Page 143
#851D – $200
#420S – $3000

Page 144
#907D – $600
#1856B – $700

Page 145
#922B – $1500
#913D – $900

Page 146
#932 – $2150
#926C – $2100

Page 147
#459D – $750
#886B – $4500

Page 148
#6217 – $150
#1062 – $100

Page 149
#1369D – $190
#6920A – $375

Page 150
#804C – $1500
#807 – $3250

Page 151
#1921 – $2950
#6668 – $145

Page 152
#80C – $800-1100
#703 – $2500-2900

Page 153
#935 – $95
#1925 – $450

Page 154
#941 D – $375
#6308C – $325

Page 155
#946 – $425
#935C – $800

Page 156
#932 – $2200
#6042 – $1500

Page 157
#1795 – $120
#942D – $5500

Page 158
#932E – $425
#6350 – $50
#2977 – $50

Page 159
#328 – $1950

Page 160
#512C – $750
#58EZ – $1250

Page 161
#534 – $1200
#2905 – $1900

Page 162
#444B – $4250
#S1667 – $2500

Page 163
$75
#9260 – $2250

Page 164
#912 – $3900
#732N – $1500

Page 165
#S1561 – $22,500
#139B – $12,000

Page 166
#1096 – $2500
#1356E – $2000

Page 167
#730 – $725
#909C – $4750

Page 168
#614F – $375
#1358D – $4000

Page 169
#129 – $2500
#6112 – $2250

Page 170
#1927 – $650
#614E – $1750

Page 171
#1654C – $7250
#704 – $7500

Page 172
#942B – $700
#1661 – $550

Page 173
#560W – $1750
#856A – $3500

Page 174
#991 – $1750
#272 – $625

Page 175
#6476 – $325
#1358 – $450

Page 176
#917A – $2000-3000
#917B – $2000-3000

Page 177
#1664D – $4000-6000
#6204B – $3000-4000

Page 178
$650
$2350

Page 179
#2511 – $375
#356F – $1500

Page 180
#2109 – $40
#1795 – $65

Page 181
#904C – $3000-3500
#S1603C – $8000-11,000

Page 182
#214B – $95
#2100 – $400

Page 183
#6319F – $35
#325E – $350

Page 184
#951C – $1000-1500
$3000-4000

Page 185
#907C – $9,000-11,000

Page 186
#1356E – $2500
#932C – $1200

Page 187
#2031 – $750

Page 188
#1929 – $850

Page 189
#935D – $2350

Page 190
#604D – $650

Page 191
#604D – $3000

Page 192
604D – $3500

Page 193
#900B – $1400

Page 194
#922C – $1000

Page 195
#1710 – $325

Page 196
#1356B – $1450

Page 197
#787C – $17,500

Page 198
#556 – $2750

Page 199
#614C – $3750

Page 200
#900C – $3900

Page 201
#1655E – $1000

Page 202
#5855 – $1300

Page 203
#6140 – $950

Page 204
#481 – $650

Page 205
#S1713 – $2450

Page 206
$400

Page 207
$7500

Page 208
$3000

Page 209
#2984A – $3500-5500

Page 210
#950C – $2500-3500

Page 211
#2786 – $2500-3500

Page 212
#85 – $1500-2500
#52 – $2000-2500
#216 – $1000-1500
#904D – $1500-2000
#218A – $2500-3500

Page 213
#560A – $2500-3000
#905C – $5000-7000
#139A – $4000-6000
#856C – $9000-11,000

Page 214
#741C – $4000-5000
$5000-7000
#860 – $2000-2500

Page 215
#800C – $1500-2000
#989D – $2000-2500
#1121C – $1500-2000
#1655 – $2000-25000

Page 216
#743C – $900-1100
#952F – $900-1200
#614D – $1000-1500
#745C – $500-700
#939D – $900-1200
#952F – $500-700

Page 217
#817 – $3000-3500
#A5 – $2000-2500
#810 – $6000-8000
#1658E – $1000-1500

Page 218
#773 – $150
#214 – $50

Page 219
#228E – $350
#214C – $800
#211 – $1250

Page 220
#214E – $750
#955 – $300
#957B – $500

Page 221
#2152 – $40
$2500-3500

Page 222
#2178B – $550
#1919 – $150

Page 223
#2364 – $750
#2510 – $450

Page 224
#2836 – $425
$725

Page 225
#6252 – $350
#6014 – $350

Page 226
#6124 – $350
#2554 – $550

Page 227
#2678 – $650
#2998 – $475

Page 228
#2655 – $425
#2653 – $325

Page 229
#2274 – $650

Page 230
#6023 – $450

Page 231
#2503 – $650

Page 232
#2732 – $650

Page 233
#598 – $2500-3000
#614 – $350

Page 234
#722 – $6000

Page 235
$275

Page 236
#3077 – $250
#3301 – $275
#3124 – $350
#3207 – $350

Page 237
#1263 – $225
#1633 – $275
#3206 – $250
#1631 – $225

Page 238
#1378 – $275
#3205 – $225
#3069 – $175
#3203 – $200

Page 239
#1794 – $300
#2043 – $350
#2047 – $195

Page 240
$200

Page 241
#7133 – $15
#7206 – $85
#2565 – $275

Page 242
$1100
#2107 – $140
#6820 – $35

Page 243
#838F – $3000
#1420 – $725
#547 – $70

Page 244
$400
#2968 – $225

Page 245
#343 – $800
#T1261 – $9500

Page 246
#479 – $1500
#1071 – $3250

Page 247
#101C – $1100
$125

Page 248
#772 – $1000
#772 – $3250

Page 249
#1171 – $350

Page 250
#5855 – $1300

Page 251
#E12 – $300
#2336 – $275

Page 252
$400
#2968 – $225

Page 253
$3000-5000

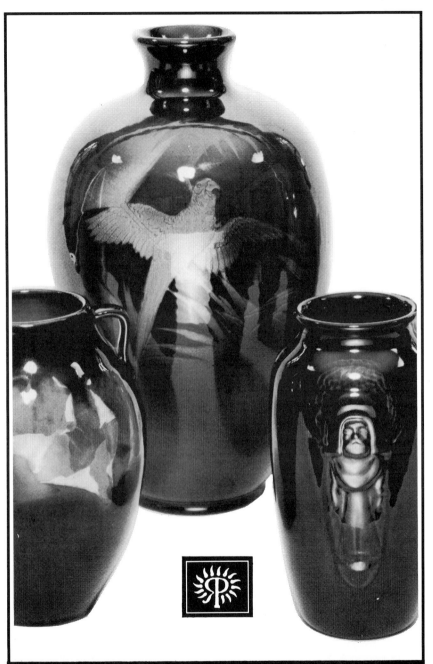

Notes

Notes

Notes